BACKPACKER'S BRITAIN
VOLUME FOUR: CENTRAL AND SOUTHERN SCOTTISH HIGHLANDS

About the Author

For over twenty years Graham Uney has been enjoying the fells and mountains of Britain. Although he currently lives in the flatlands of Hertfordshire, he spends much of his time working in the Scottish Highlands and Islands, as well as in Wales, the Lake District, and the Pennines. Work for Graham is split between writing and photographing for books and magazine features, and leading walking, wildlife and mountaineering trips for Wilderness Scotland. Graham joined the company in 2003, and is now a Senior Guide. Always at home in the hills, you might find him camping wild in the Highlands, ascending classic rock climbs of the Lake District, sailing and exploring around the Western Isles, or instructing on winter hill skills courses.

He also runs navigation, winter skills and rock climbing courses under the banner of Wild Ridge Adventure (www.wildridgeadventure.com).

Other Cicerone guides by the author
Backpacker's Britain Volume 1: Northern England
Backpacker's Britain Volume 2: Wales
Backpacker's Britain Volume 3: Northern Scotland

BACKPACKER'S BRITAIN
VOLUME FOUR: CENTRAL AND SOUTHERN SCOTTISH HIGHLANDS

by
Graham Uney

2 POLICE SQUARE, MILNTHORPE, CUMBRIA LA7 7PY
www.cicerone.co.uk

First edition 2008
ISBN-13: 978 185284 527 8
© Graham Uney 2008
A catalogue record for this book is available from the British Library.
All photographs are by the author unless otherwise stated.

Acknowledgements

As always there are countless people whom I would like to thank for either helping with this book, or for sharing with me great days out on the hills.

In particular, I must yet again thank Olivia, for encouraging my explorations of wildest Scotland.

Special thanks to Beryl and Dick Tudhope who have shared many great days in the hills with me, and many great drams back at base. I would also like to thank Janet Fisher for giving me a reason to explore both Beinn a'Bhuird and the Loch Callater hills when I might otherwise have just gone for a beer! Tim Francis also deserves a mention for always suggesting staying out that little bit later for sunset views over the Cairngorms.

I would also like to express my thanks to the staff at VisitScotland who have helped out by organising various press trips to obscure destinations.

Backpacking in Scotland throughout the year is a lot more comfortable if you have the very best equipment, and thanks to Hilleberg, I've had the use of a superb Akto tent for a while now. I hope they realise they're not likely to get it back! Paramo have also helped out enormously by providing a range of great clothing for me to test whilst out in the hills, while Berghaus and Snugpak also provided superb clothing and sleeping bags respectively. And finally, thanks to Juliet Hutton at Harvey Maps for encouraging me to look beyond the usual cartographers, and for allowing me to put their new British Mountain Maps through their paces.

Advice to Readers

Readers are advised that, while every effort is taken by the author to ensure the accuracy of this guidebook, changes can occur which may affect the contents. It is advisable to check locally on such things as transport, accommodation and shops but even rights of way can be altered.

The publisher would welcome notes of any such changes.

Front cover: Heading up Sgurr a'Mhaim from the Devil's Ridge in the Mamores

CONTENTS

Warning

Mountain walking can be a dangerous activity carrying a risk of personal injury or death. It should be undertaken only by those with a full understanding of the risks and with the training and/or experience to evaluate them. Whilst every care and effort has been taken in the preparation of this guide, the user should be aware that conditions can be highly variable and can change quickly, thus materially affecting the seriousness of a mountain walk.

Therefore, except for any liability which cannot be excluded by law, neither Cicerone nor the author accept liability for damage of any nature (including damage to property, personal injury or death) arising directly or indirectly from the information in this book.

To call out the Mountain Rescue, phone 999 or the international emergency number 112: this will connect you via any available network. Once connected to the emergency operator, ask for the police.

Map Key

A890	main road
B9078	minor road
● ● ● ● ● ●	main route
● ● ● ● ● ●	alternative route
- - - - - - -	track
🚶	start of route
🚶	finish of route
🚶	start/finish
	loch
	lighthouse
	camp
	bridge
)(	col or pass
+++++●+++++	railway/station
⬆	bothy or refuge
▲	summit
■	habitation
*	special feature
→	direction of route
	forest
	cliffs

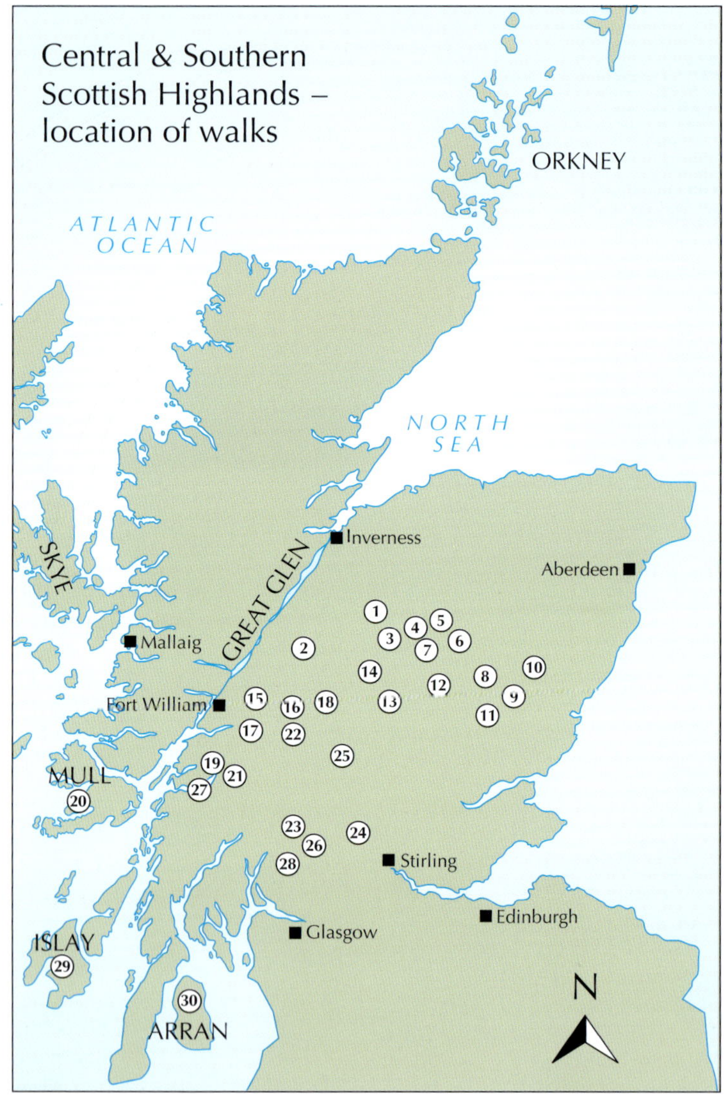

Central & Southern Scottish Highlands – location of walks
ORKNEY
ATLANTIC OCEAN
NORTH SEA
SKYE
GREAT GLEN
Mallaig
Inverness
Aberdeen
Fort William
MULL
Stirling
Edinburgh
Glasgow
ISLAY
ARRAN
N

INTRODUCTION

The mountains of Britain are one of the richest, most diverse landscapes to be found anywhere in the world. Many of our mountain and moorland regions are also within easy reach of town and city, and the Southern Highlands can be counted among them, being within a couple of hours drive from either Glasgow or Edinburgh.

Wild mountains, rocky coasts, and long, winding glens make this one of the best regions for the backpacker to explore. There are places here that take days to reach on foot, places where only the dedicated backpacker can venture. This is wilderness exploration at its best. Crossing a mountain range from one end to the other, or climbing a set of peaks around a desolate Highland glen will introduce the walker to hitherto unknown regions, and where such a trip involves the commitment of an overnight stopover or more, so much the better.

There is much to be discovered within the various mountain ranges of the Southern Highlands, but some of the coastlines and lesser hill ranges also deserve a mention, for they are just as vital a component of our natural heritage as any of the higher regions, and they can often be as grand. There is a limitless variety of possible backpacking routes, all as good as each other in terms of sense of achievement to be had from a successful trip.

The first book in this Backpacker's Britain series covered Northern England, the second covered Wales, and the third, on Northern Scotland, introduced the superb multi-day walks that could be had north of the Great Glen. This book focuses on detailed backpacking routes in some of the finest corners of Southern Scotland. Thirty routes within the boundaries of the Southern Highlands are described here, all taking two or more days to complete, with overnight stops at a bothy, youth hostel or camping, either wild or at a recognised campsite. These are in my opinion the very best backpacking walks in the region, but there is endless scope for further exploration. This should be seen only as an introduction, an aperitif perhaps, for other routes that can be planned and tackled by those who have gained experience through following the routes described here.

For the purposes of these books I have taken the boundary between Northern Scotland and Southern Scotland as being the Great Glen, that huge trench with its string of lochs stretching between Inverness on the

Beinn Fhionnlaidh from Loch Creran (Route 27)

Moray Firth in the north-east of the country to Fort William on Loch Linnhe in the west. This book features walks south of the Great Glen, and north of the Scottish central belt – the great cities of Glasgow and Edinburgh.

HOW TO USE THIS GUIDE

This book is aimed at anyone with a love of wild mountain and coastal walking. Many of the routes take the walker into remote and potentially dangerous terrain, so you should ensure that you've got prior experience of mountain walking and wild camping before tackling any of these walks. Good hill fitness is essential, as is the ability to accurately navigate using a map and compass – GPS, though a useful aid in experienced hands, is no substitute for the real thing!

The routes are ordered starting in the Monadhliath range, then going east through the Cairngorms National Park. A long multi-day route connects the Cairngorms to Lochaber, and links routes between the two areas. Most of the routes are circular, but a few are linear. They range in length from two-day routes through to a seven-day traverse.

It is hard to give a best time of year for walking in Scotland – it can be great during any season! Generally speaking midwinter (say January through to March) will give very hard conditions with most routes being snow-bound – but snow-holing instead of camping can be fun! April to June is often a really good time to be in the Highlands as the weather is often at its best then and there are fewer midges. July and August can be very hot and wet, and it is then that the midges are at their peak. September through to December can also be a great time for a backpacking trip, and most of the midges will have gone to ground by then. Note however, that you will have fewer hours of daylight in which to walk, and more time will be spent brewing up tea in tents or bothies!

Each walk begins with an **information box**. These give details of where to **start** and **finish** the walk, the **number of days** needed and the **distance** covered. The various **maps** needed along the way are also detailed here – these are the maps I feel are the most appropriate for the route, including Harvey Superwalker and/or British Mountain Maps, and/or Ordnance Survey Landranger and Explorer maps. This is subjective of course, as lots of people have their own ideas as to what makes one type of map better than another. The recommended maps are those that I found best covered the route in question.

For each route there is then an Area Summary and a Route Summary, followed by any additional information, including details of accommodation en route and local tourist information. There are also a number of suggested escape routes for each walk.

Walking towards Beinn a'Bhuird (Route 6)

Note: the sketch maps in this book are intended to be used only to show the very basic outline of the route taken. They are not intended to be used for navigational purposes while actually walking the route – it is essential that either the suggested Harvey or OS maps are used during the walk.

GETTING AROUND AND ACCOMMODATION

The Scottish Tourist Board (tel 0131 332 2433) is a great source of information when it comes to planning trips into the hills. I really couldn't have written this book without their help! Their website www.visitscotland.com is useful for booking accommodation, as well as giving useful transport information.

Accommodation needs to be planned, and often booked, ahead. You can find anything from a simple campsite, through hostels, B&Bs, guesthouses, hotels, self-catering cottages and even castles, by contacting VisitScotland. Accommodation is plentiful for most of the year, but be aware that many providers close for the winter season – from October through until March. Checking ahead is essential during this time.

For most of the routes in this book it is definitely easier if you have your own car. However, public transport is possible for many of the routes, and again VisitScotland can advise on the best way to travel to the start and finish points of each walk. A useful resource for travel information is the national organisation Traveline (tel 0871 200 2233, www.traveline.org.uk).

SAFETY IN THE HILLS

Great tomes have been written on this subject, and readers are referred to the specialist books suggested in the bibliography in Appendix 2, but for the most part, common sense is all that is required. By this I mean simply going into the hills well equipped for the task in hand, both in terms of taking the right gear with you and having the necessary navigation skills to find your way accurately in all weathers.

Many people stress the importance of leaving written word with a responsible party before heading off into the hills, and this is very good advice for those new to hillwalking. However, for me, one of the real joys of hillwalking, and backpacking in particular, is the freedom it gives, including the liberty to change plans if, for instance, you have found the going easier than expected or the weather has improved and you find yourself wanting to extend your stay in the mountains.

This is not possible, and certainly should not ever be considered, if written word of your intentions has been left. The choice is up to the individual, and whether you leave a route card or not, you should accept the responsibility that your decision imposes upon you.

Approaching the Devil's Ridge on Sgurr a'Mhaim (Route 17)

Some of the hazards to be aware of in the Scottish mountains are:

- river crossings
- cliffs
- snow fields (at certain times of the year).

Rivers can rise and fall quickly in the Highlands, and people do die trying to cross them when in spate. Not all rivers can be crossed using a bridge. Shallow water can be crossed quite easily by keeping your boots on (to avoid getting your feet crushed by moving boulders or cut on sharp rocks) and facing up stream. However, if in any doubt at all either find a way around, or camp and wait for the water level to go down.

Many of the routes in this book take you along narrow ridges and cliff tops. The dangers here are obvious.

In spring there can often be large areas of snow to cross. Carrying an ice axe and crampons is the sensible way to safely travel in the hills at this time, and it is essential that you know how to use these properly.

In an emergency mark the position of the injured person on your map. You should get to the nearest phone or house and call 999. Ask for the Police and tell them you need a Mountain Rescue. The Rescue team will come to the phone you are at and will use your map to locate the injured person.

Note that mobile phone coverage is poor in Scotland.

NAVIGATION

This is the one subject that gets people most flummoxed, or at least it is something that many hillgoers claim to have mastered, but would no doubt struggle with should push come to shove. It is beyond the scope of this book to go into any great detail, and it is hoped that anyone heading off into the hills would first book themselves onto a navigation course. Having said that, a few very general pointers are given here.

The main skill to master is that of setting the map. To oversimplify things, you need to know that the top of the map is grid north, and the red directional needle on the compass points to magnetic north. Simply put the compass onto the map and turn the map around until this needle is pointing to the top of the map. This will then set the map in line with all of the features on the ground – walls, fences, streams, hills – everything on the map will be in line with their corresponding ground features. (This is actually slightly inaccurate, as grid north and magnetic north are not exactly the same. The compass currently points slightly west of grid north in the UK at the moment, and the key at the edge of the map will tell you how many degrees the difference is for any year. You then just add that difference to the figure on the dial on your compass.)

To measure distances on the map you need to know the scale, and to measure them on the ground you need to know either how many double paces you take per 100m over different types of terrain and gradient, or how fast you are walking over the

A backpacker ready to head off up Glen Mark (Route 9)

ground. You can practise all of this by either going out with someone who already knows how to do this accurately, or by going on a navigation course.

The only true way to learn navigation is out on the hills, initially by going on a course. Cicerone Press also publish two useful skills guides on navigation: *Navigation* (2007) and *Map and Compass* (2006).

EQUIPMENT

This is a very subjective issue. A browse through any outdoor retailer's shop will reveal a bewildering array of boots, jackets, tents, sleeping bags, stoves, maps, compasses, GPS, and all sorts of gadgets that you will never need at all. In short, there is a wealth of gear and gizmos you can buy for the hills. Some of it is essential, while other bits and pieces are less so.

To get started in backpacking, you will probably find that you already possess some of the essential items – most aspiring backpackers have been active in the outdoors previously and will usually own a pair of boots, a waterproof jacket and overtrousers, and probably a compass, map case, torch and first-aid kit.

To head out for a night in the hills you will need to add a good sleeping bag to this list. There are basically two types of bag – down-filled and synthetic. Down is lighter in weight but useless if you get it wet, whereas the synthetic is heavier but retains some

of its warming properties when wet. Synthetic is usually a good deal cheaper than the better quality down-filled bag.

A good mat under your sleeping bag is essential to keep you insulated from the cold ground beneath. Foam mats are cheap, but better is a Thermarest which is air-filled. These are far more comfortable, but much more expensive.

Then you'll need a tent to put over yourself. I have used a number of different makes and models over the years, but for most people the best advice is to get the lightest tent you can for the seasons you intend to use it, and to pay the most you can afford. This latter point will automatically scrub all the next to useless models from your shopping list.

Next you'll need a stove of some sort. Gas is a popular fuel favourite, while meths-burning Trangias are very often seen being used by youth groups. The Trangia is a very safe stove and has the benefit of having no working parts to break. It is easy to light and easy to use, although it does take longer to boil water for cooking than with almost any other camping stove I have used. Personally I would always go for a Coleman Duel Fuel model. They are very efficient, and you will be drinking your soup whilst watching your main course simmer before most of your mates have even raised a bubble in their pots with other stove models.

On top of your camping equipment it is also a good idea to have

Camping in a lovely wild spot above the River Feshie (Route 14)

spare, warm, dry clothing in your rucksack for anything more than a single day in the hills.

Obviously, you'll need a larger rucksack than your daysack to carry all of this extra kit, and again, there are countless makes and models on the market. Go to an outdoor shop and try them all on, aiming for something around 60–70 litres in size. Get the assistant in the shop to fill the rucksacks for you with tents and other heavy gear, then walk around the shop to see which feels the best for you.

Once you set off on your backpack, aim to get everything into your rucksack, rather than hanging things on the outside. Apart from looking better, this also helps to distribute the weight more evenly and will make for a more enjoyable backpacking trip.

FOOD

Food should be nutritious and palatable, and you should plan to carry enough to fulfil your energy needs for the duration of the trip, plus some spare high-energy foods in case of emergency. Generally speaking most people burn 3000–4000 calories a day when they are backpacking, and it is recommended that you should replace this throughout the day – a backpacking trip is not the time to go on a diet!

Try to balance your daily intake so that you have around 60–65% carbohydrates, 25–30% fats and 10–15% protein. Plenty of fluids are essential, partly to replace that lost through sweating, and partly to help you digest food more efficiently. Try to spread your daily food intake out over the day, eating little and often throughout the walk, rather than stopping for a huge food-fest at lunchtime and spending the rest of the day snoozing it off!

It is hard to try to eat similar foods to those you would normally eat at home when on a backpacking trip. The best advice is to experiment over different trips, and this can indeed become a great part of the whole backpacking experience.

As for spare emergency food, most people throw a few chocolate bars, flapjacks or high-energy bars into the bottom of their rucksacks, but I know many people who always eat their 'emergency rations' long before the trip is over, and of course that is not ideal. Some people deliberately take with them something that they don't actually like, which is a good idea, so long as it is high in energy. I have also heard it recommended that emergency rations should be wrapped in sticky tape, making it very difficult to get into. This is fine until that emergency occurs, and then you still can't get into it!

ACCESS AND THE BACKPACKER

The Land Reform (Scotland) Act of 2003 establishes access rights for everyone to most land and inland waters, provided they exercise them responsibly. These rights and responsibilities are set out in the Scottish Outdoor Access Code. For a copy of the Code call Scottish Natural

Wild camping high on the Lochnagar plateau in winter (Route 8)

Heritage on 01738 444177, or go to www.outdooraccess-scotland.com.

Everyone has the right to be on most types of land to undertake outdoor activities such as walking, cycling, and wild camping, as long as they act responsibly. This means taking responsibility for your own actions while in the outdoors, as well as respecting the interests of other people using or working in the outdoors, and caring for the environment.

Access rights don't apply to any kind of motorised activity or hunting, shooting, or fishing. They also don't apply everywhere, and exclude buildings and their immediate surroundings, houses and their gardens,

A backpacker heading up
Glen Artney (Route 24)

Meeting the locals at Loch Ossian Youth Hostel (Route 18)

and most land in which crops are growing.

Wild Camping

Access rights extend to wild camping, which must be lightweight, done in small numbers, and not for more than two or three nights in any one location. Act responsibly by not camping in enclosed fields of crops or farm animals, and by keeping away from buildings, roads or historic structures. If you wish to camp close to a house or other building, seek the owner's permission. Leave no trace of your stay by removing all litter, and all traces of your tent pitch. Do not cause any pollution.

Neither the author nor the publisher can accept responsibility for the actions of readers of this book with regard to access on private land. The inclusion of a route in this book does not imply that the reader has a right to walk there or to camp along the route.

Stalking

Stag stalking takes place from 1 July to 20 October and hind stalking is from 21 October to 15 February. During this period you can minimise disturbance to stalking activities by finding out where stalking is taking place. Use the Hillphones service where it is available to find out which areas are out of bounds. For information and

21

area telephone numbers go to www.snh.org.uk/hillphones, or pick up a Hillphones booklet in outdoor shops, hostels, tourist information centres, or hotels.

Although the Code advises land managers to consider popular walking routes, paths and ridges when planning stalking, you should take advice on alternative routes that may be posted on signs in the area. Deer control can also take place in woodland at any time of year, often at dawn or dusk. Take extra care at these times, and again follow advice on signs locally.

WILDLIFE AND WILDFLOWERS

The wildlife and wildflowers of the Highlands are a fascinating aspect of this beautiful landscape, and are worthy of whole volumes in their own right. Following is a summary of some of the most exciting species that the backpacker might, with a watchful eye and enough patience, come across during his or her wanderings in this part of the Highlands.

Chief amongst mammals in the Highlands is the red deer. Put simply, there are far too many red deer wandering around in the hills. The lack of a natural predator is the problem – their numbers used to be kept down by the wolf, but our ancestors managed to get rid of those for us. Too few deer are being culled, and although some estates are very good at culling, numbers of deer are still increasing.

All this might sound like wonderful news, but it does mean that there simply isn't enough land to support the huge numbers at large. Many deer starve to death in the winter, but as breeding numbers are high, the population continues to grow. So, taking all this into account, you'd be very unlucky not to see some red deer while out backpacking in the wilds.

Other mammals to look out for include otters, pine marten and Scottish wildcat. Of these, otters are the one you are most likely to come across, particularly on any of the walks on the west coast islands.

Of the larger birds, ravens, buzzards and golden eagles are the most likely species. Raven numbers are decreasing, but the latter two are doing very well. Heather moorland is a good place to look for red grouse, and here you should also see curlew, snipe and golden plover in the breeding season. Mountain tops are not without wildlife either. Here you'll find snow buntings, ptarmigan and mountain hare, particularly in the Cairngorms.

In woodland you might see the secretive roe deer, while the trees attract red squirrel and many small birds. In ancient pine forests such as in Rothiemurchus there's also a chance of seeing crested tit and Scottish crossbill.

It is illegal to approach nesting birds deliberately, and it is obviously sensible not to get anywhere near deer, particularly during the rut when

On the summit of Cairn Lochain (Route 3)

the males will see you as competition. And they do have very big antlers!

Likewise, it is illegal to pick wild-flowers, and there are plenty of these to be seen in the Highlands. Of particular interest are bog asphodel, bog myrtle, ling, bell and crossed-leaved heathers, lousewort, milkwort, cow wheat and a whole range of orchids. Bilberry and crowberry can be seen on high mountain sides, and occasionally you might come across bear-berry and cowberry.

There is of course a lot of local variation, and this can make the study of the flora of Scotland particularly fascinating. While you are not likely to want to suffer the extra weight of a field guide covering flora when you're out backpacking, spending time to do a bit of research before heading out on a trip can greatly heighten the enjoyment you get when you stumble across your first cranberry, dwarf cornel, or northern marsh orchid!

A NOTE ON MEASUREMENTS

All measurements given within this book are metric, as the use of imperial measurements complicates matters enormously – all UK maps, including Harvey and OS, use metric measurements. The only exception to this is when referring to historically relevant information, such as when talking about Munros (3000'ers), Corbetts (2500'ers), and Grahams (2000'ers). This also applies to the walk over the 4000'ers of Scotland, which is a long-standing historical hillwalking challenge.

The Monadhliath from Aviemore to Kingussie

Total Distance	36km
Daily Distances	Day 1 – 23km, Day 2 – 13km
Maps	OS Landranger sheet 35 (Kingussie & Monadhliath Mountains)
Starting Point	Lynwilg (GR: NH883107), just south-west of Aviemore and on the opposite side of the A9
Finishing Point	Kingussie train station (GR: NH003756)

Area Summary

A great area for backpacking. The Monadhliath range of moorland hills lies between the Great Glen at Loch Ness, and the Spey Valley. The range has a number of Munros in the south, but the northern limits of the area are little visited, despite offering endless opportunities for exploring with a tent.

Route Summary

A superb linear route across the Monadhliath. From just outside Aviemore the first objective is the Corbett of Geal-charn Mor. A route is then followed to the north-west, down to the River Dulnain which is followed to its source, before the Corbett of Carn an Fhreiceadain is crossed on the route southwards to Kingussie.

Tourist Information

Grampian Road, Aviemore (tel 01479 810363)

Accommodation and Supplies

There are plenty of options in Aviemore. Try the Youth Hostel on Grampian Road (tel 01479 810345, website www.syha.org.uk). In Kingussie there are lots of B&Bs, but personally I would recommend the Auld Poor House (tel 01540 661558, website www.auldpoorhouse.co.uk), which lies a mile out of town northwards along the B9152.

Overnight Options
There are numerous wild campsites along the banks of the River Dulnain, while the bothy at the head of that river (GR: NH718094) is small but useful.

Escape Routes
There are various landrover tracks cutting across the Monadhliath between the River Dulnain and the Spey Valley. These form the easiest escape routes in case of bad weather or an emergency, although heading towards the Spey Valley is far preferable to making toward the Dulnain, which is a remote glen.

The views from the summit are of the Cairngorms massif across the Spey Valley to the south-east, and of the Monadhliath stretching away to the west.

DAY 1
Cross the bridge at **Lynwilg** and follow the road up the north side of the Allt na Criche until you reach the entrance to the Christian outdoor centre. Here there is a stile over a deer fence to the right, and a track climbs uphill – this is known as the Burma Road. Follow this through lovely old Scots pines to the open hillside, where the odd tree still clings here and there to the moorland flanks of **Geal-charn Mor**.

The track follows the course of the Allt Dubh, but keep far above it to the north. Follow the track around the southern flanks of Carn Dearg Mor, climbing all the way.

At the point where you have the summit of Carn Dearg Mor to the north-east you will reach a small stream with a bridge over it. Continue along the track from here for 1km, until you reach the highest point of the Burma Road. Where it levels out there is a big cairn on the highest point, and here you'll see a path running south-westwards towards the summit of Geal-charn Mor. Follow this over short-cropped sub-Arctic tundra to the summit cairn and OS trig pillar of this Corbett at 824m (GR: NH836123). ◀

Drop down to the south-west, along a narrowing ridge to **Geal-charn Beag**, then take a bearing down to **Loch a'Choin Duibh** to the west.

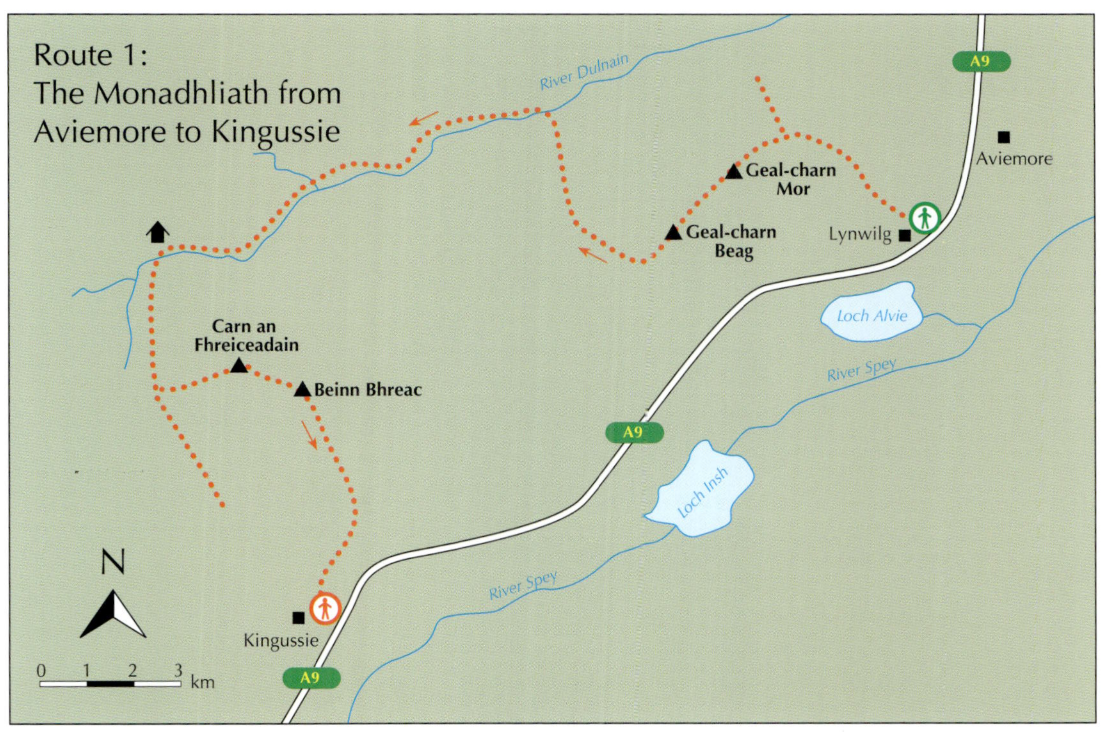
Route 1:
The Monadhliath from
Aviemore to Kingussie
River Dulnain
A9
Aviemore
Geal-charn Mor
Geal-charn Beag
Lynwilg
Loch Alvie
River Spey
Carn an Fhreiceadain
Beinn Bhreac
A9
Loch Insh
River Spey
N
0 1 2 3 km
Kingussie
A9

The track from the bothy by the River Dulnain

The ground to the west of the loch is gently undulating, and you should walk over this, **Carn an Fhuarain Duibh**, until you pick up a track cutting across the moor. Turn right along this and descend into the valley of the **River Dulnain**. Cross the Feithlinn via a footbridge, then immediately cross the River Dulnain itself to the north side. Turn upstream, to the south-west. The route now follows the river south-westwards up towards its source. You can camp along here at any number of suitable wild sites, or you can continue to the small bothy (GR: NH718094) at the head of the glen.

DAY 2

Wherever you camped the night before, make for the bothy at the head of the glen to resume the walk. Cross the river to the south and pick up a new track that climbs gently above the headwaters of the River Dulnain. The going here is easy, and you'll soon find yourself on the western flanks of your Corbett for the day, **Carn an Fhreiceadain**. If you do not wish to climb this hill, which is only a short way above you to the east, you can stay on the track which leads easily through to Kingussie.

To climb Carn an Fhreiceadain you should leave the track when you are west of the summit and follow faint paths through the heather, clambering over a little scree slope clothed with bear berries and dwarf willow. The small summit plateau is easily gained, and there is a cairn on its south-west side, while the summit is marked by an OS trig pillar at 878m (GR: NH726072). There is also the ruin of a small hut nearby on the summit plateau.

Descend eastwards to pick up a stony track. This drops to a broad col, and then takes you up and over the little mound of **Beinn Bhreac**. The track then turns to the south, and descends the broad, heathery ridge of **Bad Each**, while mountain hares scatter in all directions.

Lower down the hill you come to the banks of the Allt Mor, just before reaching **Pitmain Lodge**. Continue along the track along the east side of the Allt Mor, following it onwards as it becomes a tarmac lane. At the Kingussie Golf Club you can cross over the river via a footbridge. There is a tarmac lane on both sides of the river now, and both lead down easily to the high street in Kingussie.

At the summit of Carn an Fhreiceadain

ROUTE 2
Through Glen Roy

Total Distance	28km
Daily Distances	Day 1 – 14km, Day 2 – 14km
Maps	OS Landranger sheet 34 (Fort Augustus)
Starting Point	Melgarve (GR: NN463959), south-west of Newtonmore at the end of the public road running west from Laggan.
Finishing Point	The train station in Roybridge (GR: NN273810)

Area Summary

A wonderfully wild area for backpacking. The Monadhliath range lies between the Great Glen at Loch Ness, and the Spey Valley, running across Scotland in a south-west to north-east direction. The range has a number of important Munros in the south, which this route crosses, passing close by the northern ramparts of Creag Meagaidh.

Route Summary

A great linear route across the southern section of the Monadhliath. From Melgarve, west of Newtonmore, the route climbs to the source of the River Spey at Loch Spey, then continues westwards through to the headwaters of Glen Roy. The route then heads down Glen Roy following tracks and the quiet public road beneath the famous Parallel Roads, eventually reaching Roybridge. An easy walk suitable for those new to backpacking.

Tourist Information

There is a Tourist Information Centre in Newtonmore at the Craft Centre & Gallery on Main Street (tel 01540 673026).

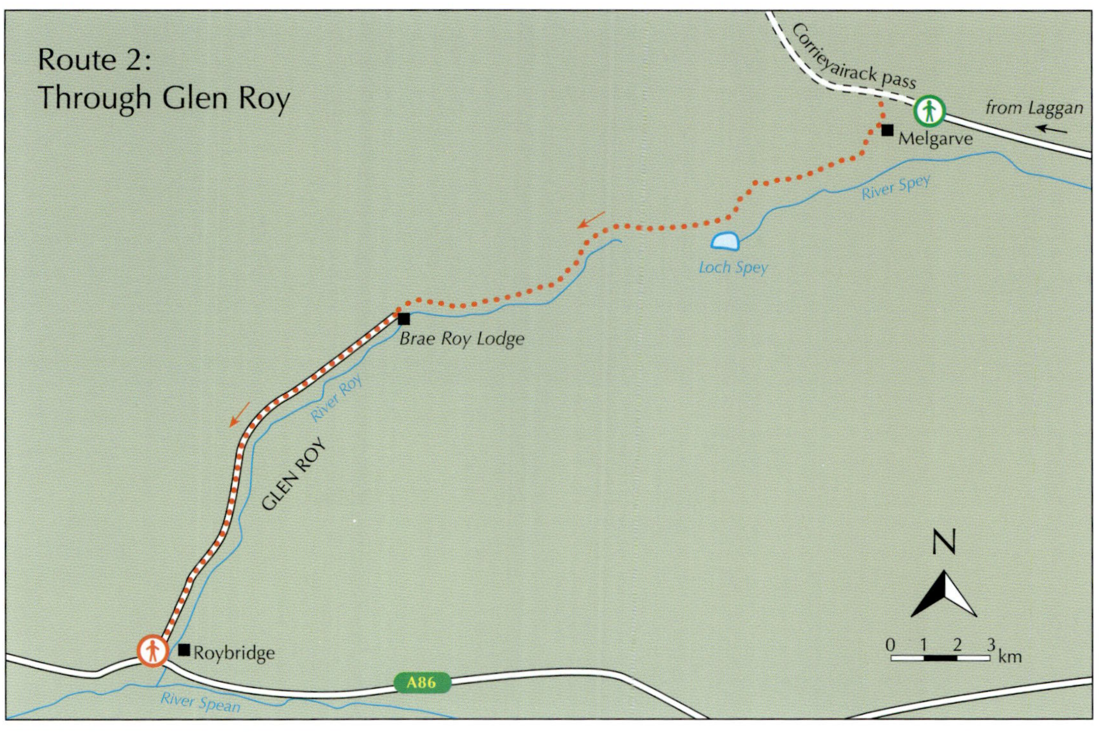

Route 2:
Through Glen Roy
Corrieyairack pass
from Laggan
Melgarve
River Spey
Loch Spey
Brae Roy Lodge
River Roy
GLEN ROY
Roybridge
A86
River Spean
N
0 1 2 3 km

Accommodation and Supplies
There are lots of options in Newtonmore. Try the Newtonmore Hostel (tel 01540 673360, www.highlandhostel.co.uk), or Strathspey Mountain Hostel, also in Newtonmore (tel 01540 673694).

Overnight Options
Camp wild at the head of Glen Roy, before you reach the end of the public road.

Escape Routes
This route is the easiest way through the mountains. Head down Glen Roy for Roybridge for the easiest route out in bad weather or in an emergency.

DAY 1

From **Melgarve** you should begin by taking the path southwards between the old buildings, aiming towards the **River Spey**. The path curves around to a plantation on the north side of the river, crossing the Allt Yairack via a bridge. It then drops down below the line of the trees in the plantation and resumes its course westwards along the riverside.

These waters are the beginnings of the mighty River Spey, and a little further on you will come to the source itself, **Loch Spey**. First, though, you need to follow the north bank of the river, leaving it briefly for Shesgnan, then dropping back southwards. The route continues westwards to the flanks of **Meall Clach a'Cheannaiche**, a low hill on the north side of the Spey. The path crosses the side of the hill at about half height, a way above the river and Loch Spey, but if you wan to visit the Loch itself you can easily drop down to its shores.

Just over 1km westwards again you'll come to a low col, an important point on this route as it marks the turning point from the eastward flowing River Spey to the westward flowing **River Roy**.

The path actually crosses over just a little way above the col, on its north side. It descends from the slopes of Meall Clach a'Cheannaiche, but not as far as the height

of the col, then heads into the wilds of **Glen Roy**.

Throughout the length of the glen the route stays on the north side of the River Roy, and initially it keeps away from the banks of the infant river. Follow it across the open meadows to **Luib-chonnal**, then walk south-west-wards to the riverside where you'll meet a big track. ▶

As you descend alongside the river you start to see evidence of the Parallel Roads.

The OS map clearly shows three sets of 'tracks' running across the contours in Glen Roy. Originally these were thought to have been made by the Gaelic legendary figure Fingal, but then in 1840 the Swiss glaciologist Louis Agassiz proposed that they were actually indicators of the levels of lakes from previous ice ages. The terraces that remain show were the lakes were trapped by the huge glaciers that filled Glen Spean and the Treig Basin. The water found its own run-off channels as the ice retreated, and so over a period of thousands of years these terraces were formed. One of the drainage channels is the col that you have crossed to get from the Spey Valley into Glen Roy.

Heading west toward Glen Roy

To the south-east the massive northern corries of Creag Meagaidh fill the scene, while the hills to the north are gentler and more rounded.

Walking down Glen Roy

A little way down the glen it is worth diverting from the track again to have a look at the Falls of Roy, and this area can be a good spot to camp for the night too.

DAY 2

Start the day by continuing down to **Leckroy**, then following the track on the north side of the river to its confluence with the **River Turret** which drains the wild hills of Teanga Mhor to the north. Cross the river via Turret Bridge, and pick up the track down to the tarmac road at Brae Roy Lodge.

Keep an eye out for red deer as you walk down the glen, as there are huge herds in these hills. This is also a good place to see golden eagles soaring along the mountain ridges on either side of the glen.

Beyond **Brae Roy Lodge** the going is easy as you are now walking on the tarmac lane. There is never much traffic, and the solid ground underfoot gives you the opportunity to watch for wildlife, and also to marvel at the Parallel Roads on either side of the glen.

You'll pass by the cottages at Achavady, Bohuntine, and Bohuntinville as you approach the woodlands of the lower glen. Then soon you'll be reaching **Roybridge** where the lane hits the A86. Turn eastwards along the lane to reach the railway station.

ROUTE 3

Glen Einich and the Great Moss

Total Distance	44km
Daily Distances	Day 1 – 23km, Day 2 – 21km
Maps	Harvey British Mountain Map 1:40,000 (Cairngorms & Lochnagar)
Starting Point	Whitewell (GR: NH916085). Turn off the main road east of Aviemore at Inverdruie, following signs for Blackpark. Turn left at Blackpark and continue to the end of the road.

Area Summary

A wild, little visited part of the Cairngorms National Park. The west side of the Braeriach plateau covers an enormous area, and there is endless scope here for long day-routes, or extended backpacking.

Route Summary

Basically a skyline traverse of Glen Einich, approaching from the north. This route follows a clockwise course taking in the summits of Braeriach, Angel's Peak, Cairn Toul, Carn Ban Mor, and Sgurr Gaoith, but could easily be extended to take in a number of other peaks nearby, including Monadh Mor, Beinn Bhrotain, and Mullach Clach a'Bhlair for those with more time. The route begins in the wonderful forests of Rothiemurchus, but soon leads onto the stark granite heights of this part of the Cairngorms.

Tourist Information

Grampian Road, Aviemore (tel 01479 810363)

Accommodation and Supplies
There are plenty of options in Aviemore. Try the Youth Hostel on Grampian Road (tel 01479 810345, website www.syha.org.uk).

Overnight Options
There are numerous wild camp sites on the plateau to the south of the head of Glen Einich.

Escape Routes
The Lairig Ghru to the east and Glen Feshie to the west are always good options, or you could head out via Glen Einich, taking the path off the plateau to the west of Carn na Criche (GR: NN926979).

DAY 1
From the car parking area at the end of the road there's a muddy little path that leads east. Follow this downhill a short way until you come across a much broader and less muddy track. Turn right along this and walk into the forest, with the whole of the Glen Einich hills spread out before you. In half a kilometre you'll reach a junction – go straight ahead here to another junction at Lochan Deo, and continue straight ahead here too. The path skirts the edge of the old Caledonian pine forests, and leads up into the magnificent heart of the Glen Einich mountains.

You can continue right up into the head of the glen, picking up a path that leads up onto the **Braeriach** plateau just west of Carn na Criche, but to avoid having to back-track to gain the summit of Braeriach it is better to take the path alongside the stream known as the **Beanaidh Bheag**, 5km from Lochan Deo.

This path is a little vague in places, but if you stay alongside the stream throughout you'll eventually find yourself in the rough cirque of Coire Beanaidh high up under the northern flanks of Braeriach's summit. There are various ways onto the plateau from the upper corrie, but the easiest way with a big backpack is via the south-eastern exit, heading up a broad gully to a col

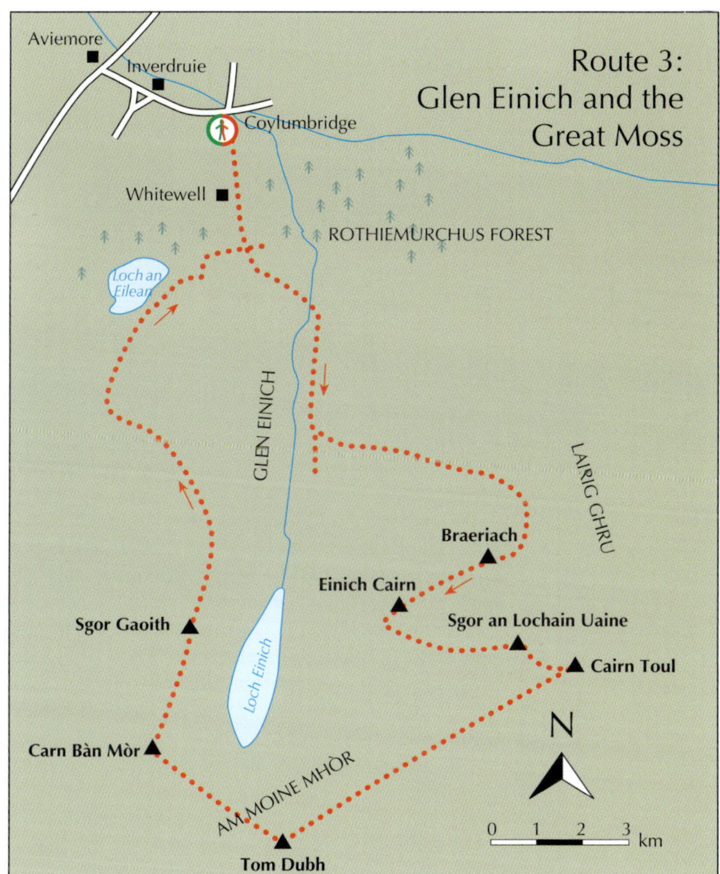

(GR: NH963003), just south of **Sron na Lairig**.

Head east a short way for spectacular views down into the Lairig Ghru, then south-westwards to pick up the path leading towards the summit of Braeriach. The path skirts the edge of the cliffs falling into Coire Bhrochain to the south, and you should handrail along this edge westwards to the summit cairn at 1296 metres.

Braeriach

Immediately south-west of the summit is a rocky gully cutting into the plateau, and you should go around this then head west across the open plateau to the small cairn on Stob Coire an Lochain at 1235m. Taking another compass bearing to the south-west you'll walk quite close to the edge of the drop into the head of Glen Einich, and it is worth making the detour for the views down onto the Loch deep in the corrie bowl. **Einich Cairn** is another important landmark on this vast plateau, and as the name suggests, the top, at 1237m, is marked by a cairn.

The Wells of Dee rise just south-east of the top, and this is a superb place to stop for a brew-up, drinking water from the source of the mighty river. Heading on, it is best to go eastwards to regain the rim of the corrie on the east side of the plateau, for from here the views are best, sweeping down into the rugged expanse of An Garbh Choire. Across the corrie to the south-east the lovely cone of Sgor an Lochain Uaine, or Angel's Peak, rises atop a scattering of slabs and boulders.

To get to the summit of **Sgor an Lochain Uaine**, you'll have to continue around the rim of the plateau, first south-west, then south, then eastwards, keeping the cliffs of Garbh Choire Mor close by as a guide all the way. ▶

Slightly higher than Sgor an Lochain Uaine is **Cairn Toul**, lying a short way off to the south-east. Drop down into the col between the two, then climb easily up to the summit at 1291m.

Well, that's the classic Munros traverse done and dusted. Now for the wild wastes of the Moine Mhor – or the 'Great Moss'.

Am Moine Mhor is the huge expanse of upland plateau lying to the west of the great peaks of Braeriach and Cairn Toul. It is a wild region, and one little visited by walkers, who generally just skirt its edges as they ascend the Munros on it periphery.

From Cairn Toul you should head south-westwards, being careful not to be drawn too far downhill as you walk across the headwaters of the Allt Clais an t-Sabhail. The exact route you should take really depends upon where you intend to camp for the night. It's possible to camp by the lonely **Loch nan Stuirteag** (GR: NN941958), but other options are **Loch nan Cnapan** (GR: NN917960), or even the lofty summit of **Tom Dubh** (GR: NN922953), at a height of 918m. There is a vast plateau of opportunities out there for you to discover!

DAY 2

Wherever you spent the night, the starting point for the second day has to be the summit of Tom Dubh – one of the lesser known summits of the Cairngorms.

From Tom Dubh's little top walk north-westwards over rough, hummocky ground, following the course of the Allt Sgairnich to the broad summit slopes of **Carn Bàn Mòr**. The top is marked by a cairn at 1052m.

Northwards there is a long, sweeping ridge, with the deep **Glen Einich** to its east and the deeply wooded Glen

Sgor an Lochain Uaine is a fabulous peak, and its summit at 1258m is a great place to relax for a while and enjoy the views back across the corrie to Braeraich.

The ridges of Braeriach across the Lairig Ghru from Lurcher's Crag

Feshie to the west. There are a number of tops along this ridge, but only one makes it into Munro's Tables: **Sgor Gaoith**, or 'Peak of the Winds'. This Munro has a magnificent position on the very crest of the crags falling in broken ridges and gullies down to the shores of **Loch Einich**. Head northwards along a vague path, veering slightly to the east to pick up the handrail along the rim of the crags. Sgor Gaoith's summit is marked by a cairn at 1118m, and in clear weather is never in doubt. In mist, however, the whole of Am Moine Mor can be a very confusing place.

From Sgor Gaoith's top continue along the broad ridge northwards, taking in the top of **Sgoran Dubh Mor** before dropping down the flanks of Sgoran Dubh Beag.

The onwards connecting ridge undulates before the rise to **Clach Mhic Cailein**, or the Argyll Stone. Still the views down to the east are dominated by Glen Einich, while the forests of Glen Feshie now beckon to the west.

Walk north-west to pick up the stream known as the Allt Coire Follais, following this down to the glen bottom near Inshriach. Here you meet a big track cutting along the glen. Turn right and follow this track to the southern tip of **Loch an Eilean** where the track splits. Both ways circle the loch, but for the shortest return to Whitewell take the right fork around the south-east shores of the loch. At the far eastern extremes of Loch an Eilean there is another junction, and here you should turn right, following the track to Lochan Deo, the small loch that you passed yesterday at the foot of Glen Einich. Turn left and follow your outwards steps back to **Whitewell**.

ROUTE 4
Through the Lairig Ghru

Total Distance	30km (Coylumbridge to Linn of Dee)
Daily Distances	Day 1 – 17km, Day 2 – 13km (to the Linn of Dee car park – it's a further 2.5km to Inverey, and another 7km to Braemar).
Maps	Harvey British Mountain Map 1:40,000 (Cairngorms & Lochnagar)
Starting Point	Coylumbridge (GR: NH914107). Park on the roadside by the campsite in Coylumbridge (if you stay here overnight at the start/end of your walk, they may let you leave your car on the site).
Finishing Point	Linn of Dee car park (GR: NO063897), west of Braemar.

Area Summary

A wild, but well-known part of the Cairngorms National Park. The great trench of the Lairig Ghru cuts right through the Cairngorm massif, separating the Ben Macdui group of mountains to the east of the pass from the Braeriach group to the west.

Route Summary

A classic route through one of the best known passes in the Highlands. The Lairig Ghru connects the Spey valley with Deeside, and has been used as a major crossing point of the mountains for thousands of years. It can be done by the very fit in a day, although to get the most from the experience, two days should be allowed. The route starts in the lovely forests of Rothiemurchus, then crosses the high and exposed pass of the Lairig Ghru before continuing down to Deeside. This is a linear route, and you will need to arrange transport at each end, or perhaps combine this route with a return over the Lairig an Laoigh (Route 5) for a superb multi-day expedition.

Tourist Information
Grampian Road, Aviemore (tel 01479 810363)

Accommodation and Supplies
There are plenty of options in Aviemore. Try the Youth Hostel on Grampian Road (tel 01479 810345), or better still, the campsite in Coylumbridge (tel 01479 812800, website www.rothiemurchus.net). The Youth Hostels at Braemar (tel 01339 741659), or Inverey (tel 01339 741017) are good places to stay at the end of the walk (website www.syha.org.uk).

Overnight Options
Lots of good options for camping wild through the Lairig Ghru, and also a recently refurbished bothy at Corrour (GR: NN981957).

Escape Routes
The Lairig Ghru itself is the only easy way through these mountains – all other routes involve heading onto the plateaux on either side and can't be considered as escape routes.

DAY 1
To the right of the entrance to the Rothiemurchus Campsite at **Coylumbridge** there is a path leaving the B970 and heading south into the Caledonian forest. Begin by taking this path, enjoying the wonderful primeval forests as you go. After 700m you'll reach a junction – take the fork to the left, which runs quite close to the river.

When we talk about the ancient forests that once cloaked Britain, we tend to think of dense and lush woodlands. This was not actually the case – the original woodlands of Britain were often quite open, with a mix of species. Here in the Rothiemurchus Forest the species are those you'd expect to find in a native woodland – predominantly Pinus sylvestris, or Scots pines (the Scots themselves call these Caledonian pines), along with a scattering of birch, alder, and rowan.

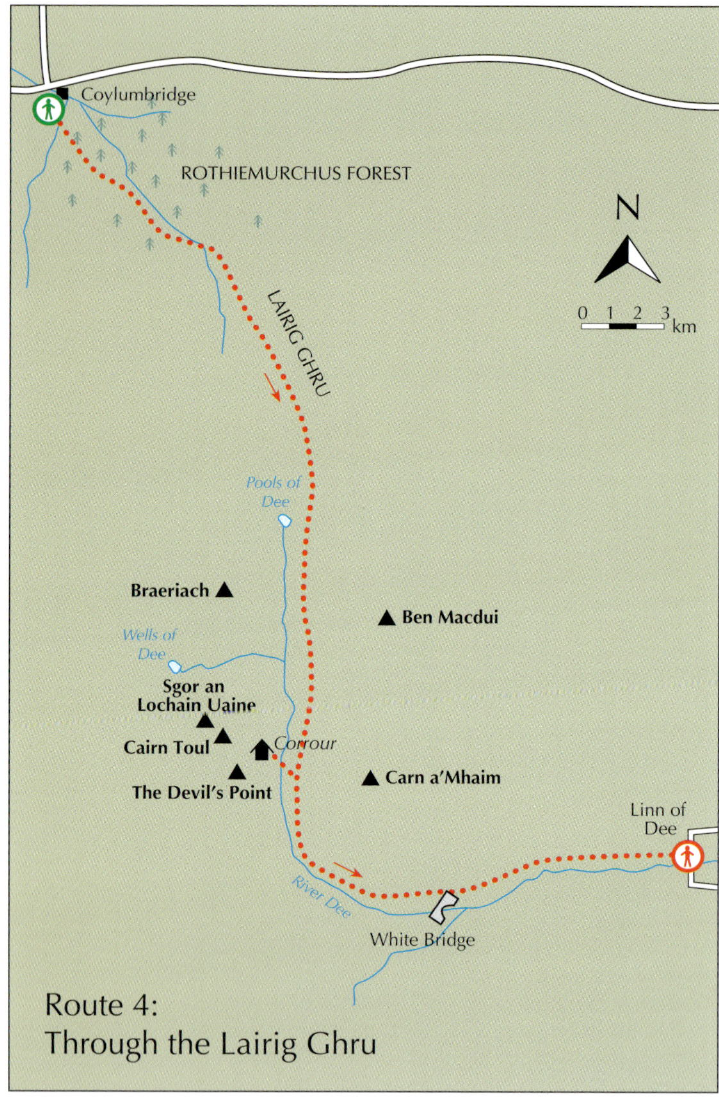

Route 4:
Through the Lairig Ghru

Ignore the next fork on the right, just before you reach a footbridge over the river on the left. This is the Cairngorm Club Footbridge, and it gives access to the lower parts of the **Lairig Ghru**. Cross over and turn right, following the river until it bends away. Stay on the path as it curves to the left at an old ruin. You soon reach a crossroads by a big cairn. Turn right here and continue, coming back along the river as it gushes out from the Lairig Ghru dead ahead. ▶

The main climbing begins here, following the path throughout, a little rough and bouldery in places, but generally very easy underfoot.

As you gain more height the Lairig becomes hemmed in between the huge mountains of the Cairngorms. To your left is **Creag an Leth-choin** (usually just known as Lurcher's Crag), which is the extension of the long ridge running north-west from Ben Macdui (the second highest mountain in Scotland, after Ben Nevis). To your right is **Sron na Lairig**, which is the north-east ridge of Braeriach (the second highest mountain in the Cairngorms, after Ben Macdui).

The path takes you across the Allt Druidh, the stream that has been your guide since leaving Coylumbridge, and continues climbing to the top of the pass (GR: NH973013).

As you get to the top of the pass the views begin to open up to the south, down over the length of the River Dee, and just over the other side of the pass you'll find the **Pools of Dee**, one of the sources of the river that continues out to the North Sea at Aberdeen.

The path to the Pools of Dee is rough, but as you begin to descend on the south side of the Lairig the way becomes easier. The path keeps to the east side of the River Dee throughout.

Continue for 2km from the top of the pass, where you will get an awesome view into Braeriach's Garbh Choire to the west. **Braeriach** lies to the right hand side

Now the trees begin to thin out, and you are looking right into the enormous trench of the Lairig Ghru.

The Lairig Ghru from Whitewell

of the corrie, while to the left are the wonderful pointed peaks of **Sgor an Lochain Uaine** (Angel's Peak), and **Cairn Toul**.

Continue down the broad valley of the Lairig Ghru, keeping an eye out for the **Corrour** bothy on the west side of the River Dee – there is a bridge over the river, and a path leads down to this from a crossroads just south of the bothy. The bothy itself sits beneath the vast slabs of **The Devil's Point**, and you may want to consider using it for an overnight stop. Failing that there are plenty of great places to camp, either nearby or further on downstream.

DAY 2

At the footpath junction (GR: NN986954) on the east side of the River Dee, just across from Corrour bothy, take the downhill path to the south-west. This drops slightly towards the river.

The uphill path to the south-east leads over a broad col between Carn a'Mhaim and Sgor Mor, taking you to the Linn of Dee through Glen Luibeg. This is a slightly shorter route, and is very beautiful, but it leaves the main Lairig Ghru path – it makes a fine alternative nevertheless.

The Lairig Ghru path keeps to the east bank of the River Dee, sometimes coming very close to it as you round the western flanks of **Sgor Mor**. Stay on the path throughout, to **White Bridge** (GR: NO019884). Then, keeping to the north side of the River Dee and walking eastwards, follow the track through to the **Linn of Dee**.

To get to Inverey or Braemar, turn right on the road, over the bridge, and continue on the south side of the River Dee.

To connect with Route 5, turn left at the Linn of Dee to the car park where that route starts.

Looking southwards through the Lairig Ghru from Lurcher's Crag

ROUTE 5
The Lairig an Laoigh

Total Distance	32km
Daily Distances	Day 1 – 16km, Day 2 – 16km
Maps	Harvey British Mountain Map 1:40,000 (Cairngorms & Lochnagar)
Starting Point	Linn of Dee car park (GR: NO063897), west of Braemar.
Finishing Point	Glenmore Forest Park (GR: NH977097), east of Aviemore.

Area Summary

A lovely, remote part of the Cairngorms National Park. Lots of walkers come to this area, mainly to access the Munros of Derry Cairngorm, Beinn Mheadhoin, and Bynack More. The Lairig an Laoigh itself is relatively popular, but nowhere near as often walked as the Lairig Ghru. The Lairig an Laoigh is the main pass route through the eastern side of the Cairngorms, running between the main Ben Macdui/Cairngorm massif, and the mountains of Beinn a'Bhuird and Ben Avon.

Route Summary

The route follows the east bank of the River Lui to Derry Lodge, then takes you northwards up Glen Derry to Dubh Lochan. Just beyond there is a river crossing at the Fords of Avon, with a small shelter on the north side. The Lairig an Laoigh rises to the north of the Fords of Avon, and the route follows this around the eastern side of Bynack More, curving around to Bynack Stables and eventually the Pass of Ryvoan. Glenmore is then an easy walk to the south-west.

Tourist Information
Braemar TIC (tel 01339 741600)

Accommodation and Supplies
There are plenty of options in Braemar. The Youth Hostels at Braemar (tel 01339 741659), or Inverey (tel 01339 741017) are good places to stay (website www.syha.org.uk).

Overnight Options
Lots of good options for camping wild through the Lairig an Laoigh, and also a (pretty grim) shelter at the Fords of Avon (GR: NJ042031).

Escape Routes
The Lairig an Laoigh is the only easy way through these mountains – all other routes involve heading onto the plateaux on either side and can't be considered as escape routes.

DAY 1

From the back corner of the car park at **Linn of Dee** there's a faint path leading northwards then curving right over a stream. Follow this path until it hits the main track leading up the glen. Turn left at this junction and follow the main track up the west side of the **Lui Water**. A kilometre from the junction the track leads down to the river and crosses over via a bridge. Immediately over the bridge you'll find another track junction. Turn left here and continue up the glen, now with the river to your left. Follow this broad valley to the lovely woodlands around **Derry Lodge**. There are a number of tracks heading into the hills from Derry Lodge, but to keep towards the Lairig an Laoigh, do not cross the bridge, just turn right at the lodge and keep to the east side of the main river. ▶

Continue up the east side of the wide glen of Glen Derry, passing great stands of Scot's pines. Ignore the track on the left which leads down to a bridge over the river and goes back to Derry Lodge.

The route passes between the peaks of **Beinn Bhreac** to the east and **Derry Cairngorm** to the west, and at this

The track now takes you up into the heart of Glen Derry, where red deer stags roam amongst the trees, and crossbills flit through the branches.

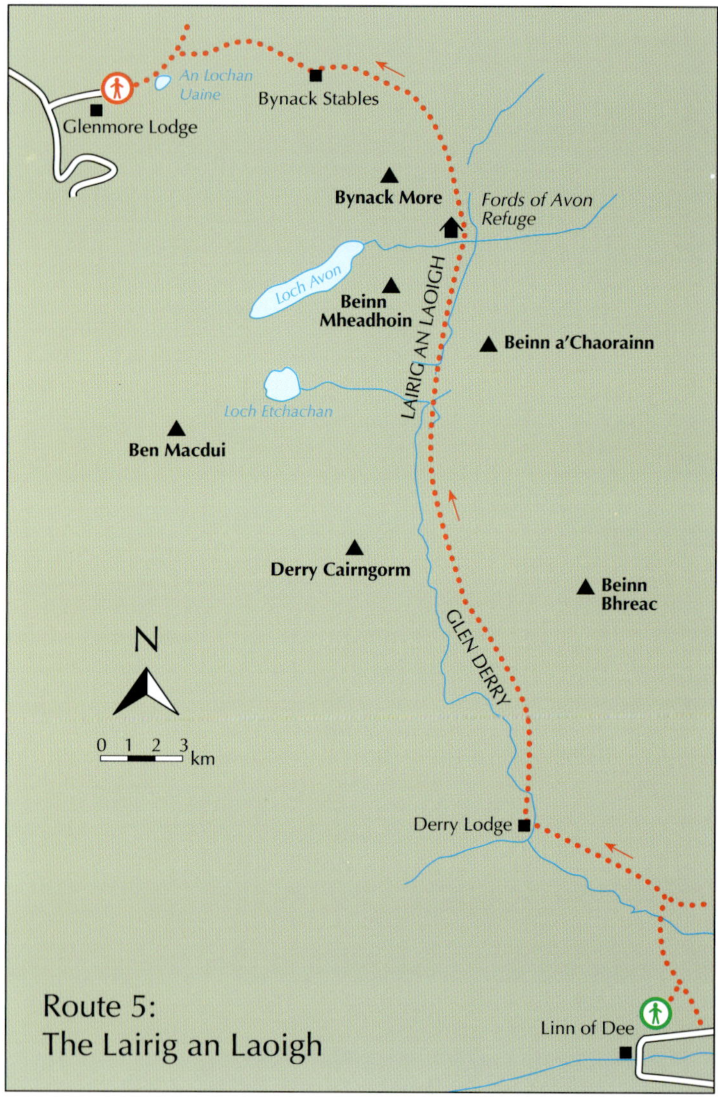

Route 5:
The Lairig an Laoigh

At the Fords of Avon Refuge

point you pass through a small plantation. Continue 800m beyond the plantation to cross a side stream, then in another 350m you will come to a path junction. Ignore the path leading off to the left, as this heads off into the wilderness area around Loch Etchachan. Instead take the path going north, climbing diagonally across the lower south-western slopes of **Beinn a'Chaorainn**. This takes you up a 150m ascent to a col (GR: NJ033004) between Beinn a'Chaorainn and **Beinn Mheadhoin**, and once there, at 746m you may be tempted to nip up either of these two Munros. Beinn a'Chaorainn is the easiest of the two, although Beinn Mheadhoin is not too difficult either. You could of course leave your rucksack on the col, and climb both hills, returning via the same route as your ascent.

It is not necessary to climb either peak of course. From the col the path leads northwards down the other side, dropping steadily down the east side of the stream that drains into the **Dubh Lochan**. Pass to the right of the Dubh Lochan, following the path over the stream issuing from this small lake. Cross a flat area of ground to the **Fords of Avon** (pronounced Aan). This can be impassable at times of spate, so be careful. If at all in doubt just camp up for the night and wait for the water level to drop before crossing.

On the north side of the river is the tiny Fords of Avon Refuge, but this is little more than a hollowed-out cairn, and is not an ideal place to spend the night. However, it is a useful shelter in emergencies.

DAY 2

To the north of the Fords of Avon Refuge the **Lairig an Laoigh** continues, cutting a trench between the Munro, **Bynack More**, and the Corbett, **Creag Mhor**.

Continuing north from the refuge, after 200m the path crosses the Allt Dearg, then follows it up its east side to the top of the pass. At the highest point (726m) there is a small tarn, Lochan a'Bhainne. From here it is possible to bag a couple more hills – you could climb Bynack More to the north-west, or the smaller Creag Mhor to the east.

Continuing from the Lairig an Laoigh the path drops 30m, then crosses the stream to the north. The path here does not continue down the valley formed by the Glasath, but instead forces a way across the open moorland to the north of Bynack More.

Walk northwards to a broad shoulder at the spot height 776m, then curve across **Coire Odhar**, over the headwaters of the Uisige Dubh Poll a'Choin, heading north-westwards along the path to the flat moorlands to the north of Bynack More.

Once on this flat plateau you'll come across the main path coming down off Bynack More's north ridge – the route used by the majority of the Munro-baggers climbing that hill.

The route continues to the north-west, dropping downhill in a broad curve to cross the **River Nethy** at the bridge at the old **Bynack Stables** (GR: NJ021105). ◀

The track from here is very wide and takes you through lovely heather moorland – look for both red grouse and black grouse as you walk.

The Barns of Bynack

Once beyond Loch a'Garbh-choire, which lies just down the slopes to your right, the track bends around to the south-west to enter the Pass of Ryvoan ('the Thieves Pass'). As you descend you'll notice another track coming in from the right. Ignore this and turn left, heading into the deep pass itself.

At the middle point of the pass you'll see the wonderfully green **An Lochan Uaine** tucked into the hollow at the bottom of the steep scree slopes of Creag nan Gall. Ignore all side paths now and just continue on the main track running out of the glen to the south-west. This track leads to the road end at **Glenmore Lodge** (you could pop in to the bar here for a celebratory drink!). On the north side of the public road (heading west) there is a path that runs parallel to the road. Follow this to Glenmore itself where you can catch buses into Aviemore.

ROUTE 6
The Eastern Cairngorms

Total Distance	44km
Daily Distances	Day 1 – 24km, Day 2 – 20km
Maps	Harvey British Mountain Map 1:40,000 (Cairngorms & Lochnagar)
Starting Point	Linn of Quoich car park (GR: NO117910), on the north side of the River Dee, west of Braemar. Note, the car park shown on the maps as being to the east of the bridge at Linn of Quoich is closed. There is a large parking area just west of the bridge.

Area Summary

One of the wildest parts of the Cairngorms, these hills offer any number of superb routes for the backpacker, with countless lovely glen routes, as well as opportunities for climbing some of the most remote Munros in Scotland. The mountains here rise to the north of the River Dee. Approaches to the peaks are long, and so the backpacker definitely has the advantage here.

Route Summary

A traverse of the high peaks of the Eastern Cairngorms. From the Linn of Quoich a route is followed up Glen Quoich until Beinn Bhreac can be climbed. The wild plateau to the north is then crossed to Beinn a'Chaorainn, before the long and lonely wilderness towards Beinn a'Bhuird is taken on. A wild camp in one of the high corries of this vast mountain gives easy access onto Ben Avon on the second day.

DAY 1

Just between the parking area and the bridge at **Linn of Quoich** there is a path that slants up the hill, directly behind the car park. Begin by following this uphill, to

Tourist Information
Braemar TIC (tel 01339 741600)

Accommodation and Supplies
There are plenty of options in Braemar. The Youth Hostels at Braemar (tel 01339 741659), or Inverey (tel 01339 741017) are good places to stay (website www.syha.org.uk).

Overnight Options
Camp wild anywhere on the plateau, or get tucked into Coire nan Clach (GR: NJ099001) on Beinn a'Bhuird for a cosy night in one of Britain's most remote corries.

Escape Routes
Head for Glen Quoich where a series of paths and tracks lead out to the Linn of Quoich. Heading south from any point on this route will lead eventually to one of the glens running into Deeside. Escape routes here though are going to be long and hard in any direction.

where it curves around to the north-west to join a bigger track. At this junction turn right and follow the main track north-westwards up the west side of **Glen Quoich**.

After 5km (from the car park) there is a path coming down from the left, just before a stream. Ignore this path and cross the stream. Immediately after crossing over this turn left on a path that leads west, then south-westwards up a narrowing gully beneath Clais Fhearnaig. Walk past a series of long, narrow lochans, then at the highest point of the gully turn northwards and climb heathery slopes to the summit of **Meall an Lundain** at 777m (GR: NO063948).

Take a bearing north-westwards down to the col at 673m, then follow another bearing north-eastwards to the stony summit of **Beinn Bhreac** (GR: NO058971), which at 931m is the first Munro of the trip. ▶

It is a 4.4km walk, directly over largely featureless terrain, to **Beinn a'Chaorainn**. Start by heading north-west down to the Moine Bhealaidh, then northwards for

A vast and empty landscape lies to the north, so careful navigation is needed to get safely across to the next summit in all but the clearest of weather.

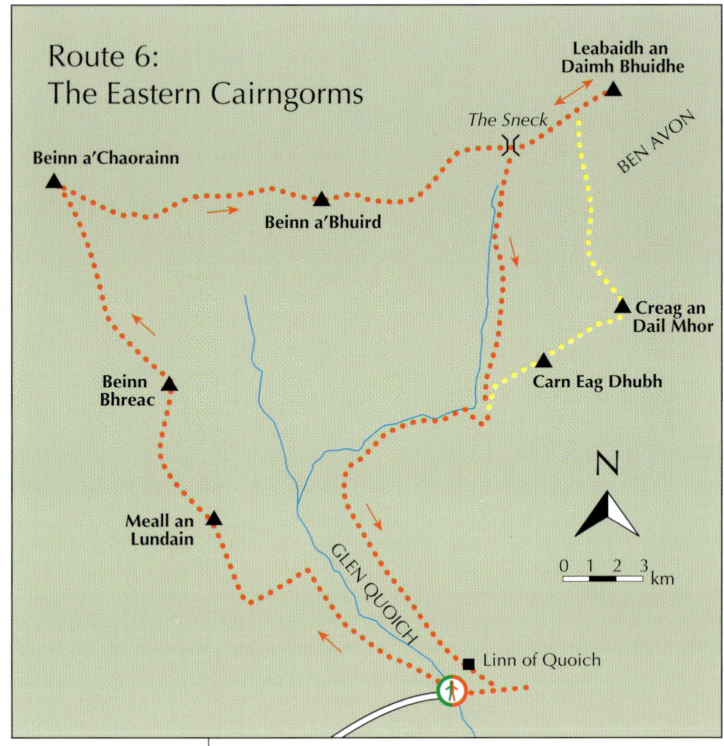

1km until you are in a broad bowl. From here it is an easy ascent north-westwards to the top of the second Munro, Beinn a'Chaorainn, (GR: NJ045014) at 1083m.

The way from here again crosses a huge and wild area of plateau. With the broad slopes of **Beinn a'Bhuird** ahead throughout you certainly have a great goal for which to aim. Start by heading south east for 2.2km to the very broad col (GR: NJ064003) at 831m, between Beinn a'Chaorainn and Beinn a'Bhuird. From the col it is straightforward to the North Top of Beinn a'Bhuird at 1197m. Just follow a bearing up the broad and easy-angled slopes to the small summit cairn (GR: NJ093006).

The views from the summit are a little restricted by the convex nature of the slopes, but if you walk 100m to the south-east you get a spectacular glimpse into the bowels of **Coire nan Clach**. Down in this wild corrie you'll see a little lochan – a good place to camp for the night.

To get down to the lochan, however, requires a little deviousness, as the direct descent is very steep and rocky. Walk eastwards along the rim of the cliffs, handrailing along for 1.5km until you are clear of the cliffs. There is a stream at this point, and you can descend alongside this for 75m until you can cut back beneath the cliffs to the lochan (GR: NJ099001).

A backpacker resting on the way up Beinn a'Bhuird

There are countless other possibilities for camping wild on these broad hills. If the weather is fine, a camp on the plateau itself is a memorable way of spending the night.

DAY 2

Start the day with a dip in the lochan and a brew-up of tea! (Just a suggestion …)

Leave the camp spot and retrace your steps, heading eastwards back beneath the cliffs until you reach the stream.

The key to gaining the next Munro, **Ben Avon**, is the col known as **The Sneck** (GR: NJ118010). To reach this

The summit plateau of Beinn a'Bhuird in winter

you can either walk up hill, skirting around the east side of Cnap a'Chleirich until you reach the edge of the cliffs falling northwards into **Garbh Choire**. From there you should just turn right and handrail along the top edge of these cliffs until you get to The Sneck.

The other way of getting there is to traverse around, following the 970m contour which is just above the height of your camp, and which is the exact height of the col. There's always a tendency to veer off downhill when contouring – or else overcompensate by climbing instead! If you can stay on the said contour throughout the traverse you're doing well.

From The Sneck climb stony slopes eastwards, keeping the cliffs of the Garbh Choire close by to your left throughout. Go over one broad bump on the Ben Avon Plateau, then continue north-eastwards to the summit (GR: NJ133018), a granite tor at 1171m giving an easy scramble to the top. The summit itself is known as **Leabaidh an Daimh Bhuidhe**, but the entire mountain goes under the name of Ben Avon.

There are various routes you can take back into Glen Quoich. The Sneck itself lies right at the very head of the glen, and you could retrace your steps as far as that col, then descend southwards on the path to **Clach a'Chleirich** ('the Cleric's Stone'). From the Clach follow the path along the east bank of the Quoich Water to a junction of paths (GR: NO117967). The following is an alternative route south from the Ben Avon summit over the plateau, which will bring you to the same path junction.

If the weather is good it is worth exploring the plateau a little before descending. There are numerous granite tors thrusting out of the gravely ground, and you can have a fun time scrambling around them.

The high-level descent leaves the summit of Leabaidh an Daimh Bhuidhe by taking you south-westwards to the minor top known as Carn Eas (GR: NO123993). From there you can descend, easily at first then with increasing steepness, to the col at 907m (GR: NO129985). Climb to the summit of **Creag an Dail Mhor** at 972m for superb views back across the plateau to Ben Avon, and westwards into the rugged corries of Beinn a'Bhuird.

Descend south-westwards to a junction of paths (GR: NO117967) low down in Glen Quoich. This is the same junction as is reached via the descent from The Sneck.

Continue southwards on the path for 700m, then zigzag downhill to the west to pick up a vague path that runs westwards along the south bank of the Quoich Water. This passes through some lovely areas of Caledonian pine. The path soon becomes more obvious, and swings southwards, high above the glen, taking you back to the **Linn of Quoich** to the east of the bridge. Once on the tarmac road, turn west over the bridge to return to your car.

ROUTE 7
The Cairngorms High Level Traverse

Total Distance	69km
Daily Distances	Day 1 – 19km, Day 2 – 13km, Day 3 – 13km, Day 4 – 24km
Maps	Harvey British Mountain Map 1:40,000 (Cairngorms & Lochnagar)
Starting Point	Linn of Dee car park (GR: NO063897), west of Braemar

Area Summary

The Cairngorms are the only area of sub-Arctic tundra in Britain. This vast wilderness of high mountain plateau is a wonderful region for exploring with a backpack. Be warned however, that the region also gets the harshest weather conditions in the country, and it can snow – even blizzard conditions are possible – on any day of the year up here. Keep a weather eye out, and pick a settled period for this traverse of the highest peaks of the Cairngorms National Park.

Route Summary

A superb traverse of all of the 4000ft peaks of the Cairngorms, plus many other lower peaks too. From the south side of the Cairngorms National Park the route takes in Ben Avon, Beinn a'Bhuird, Beinn a'Chaorainn, Cairngorm, Ben Macdui, Braeraich, Angel's Peak, and Cairn Toul, in a magnificent four-day backpack. Some people may wish to try to do this in a short time, while others may want to take longer.

Tourist Information
Braemar TIC (tel 01339 741600)

Accommodation and Supplies
There are plenty of options in Braemar. The Youth Hostels at Braemar (tel 01339 741659), or Inverey (tel 01339 741017) are good places to stay (website www.syha.org.uk).

Overnight Options
The options for wild camps are endless, while the bothy at Corrour (GR: NN981957), and the refuges at the Fords of Avon (GR: NJ042031), and in Braeriach's An Garbh Coire (GR: NN959986) may also be found useful. **Note**: these refuges are very basic stone shelters – not Alpine-style huts!

Escape Routes
This is very remote country, and any escape routes are going to be long and arduous. The glens usually provide the best routes out in bad weather or an emergency – Glen Quoich, Glen Lui, and the Lairig Ghru are the best escape routes to the south, while the Lairig an Laoigh, Strath Nethy, Lairig Ghru, Glen Einich, and Glen Feshie are the best routes out to the north and west.

DAY 1
From the back corner of the car park at **Linn of Dee** you'll find a faint path leading northwards, then bending around to the right over a small stream. Follow this path until it hits the main track leading up the glen. Turn left at this junction and follow the main track up the west side of the **Lui Water** for 1km, until the track leads down to the river and crosses over via a bridge. Immediately over the bridge you'll find another track junction. Turn left here and continue up the glen, this time with the river to your left. Continue up Glen Lui for 1km, until you reach the first stream on your right. Here there is another path junction, and you should climb uphill to the north-east into a narrow trench cutting across the hills below **Clais Fhearnaig**. Walk right through this trench, passing a number of narrow lochans, and drop down the other side into **Glen Quoich**. You'll come to the main track up Glen Quoich at the bottom of the hill. Turn left here along the track, fording the river a little way further on.

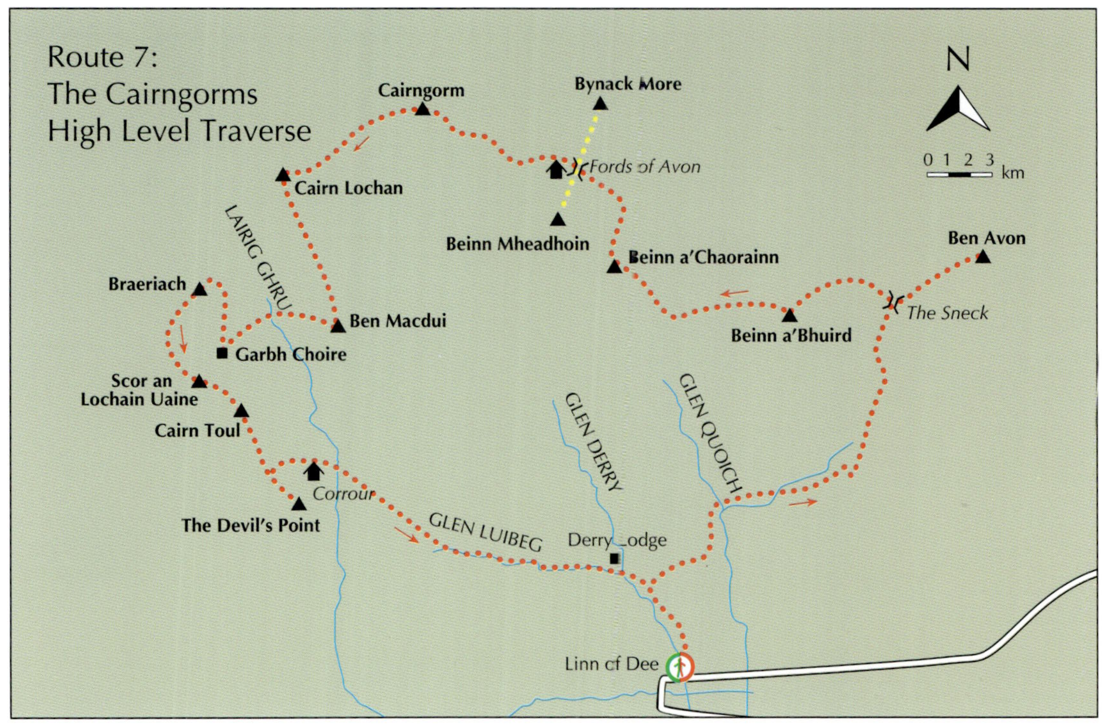

Route 7:
The Cairngorms
High Level Traverse
N
0 1 2 3 km
Cairngorm
Bynack More
Cairn Lochan
Fords of Avon
Beinn Mheadhoin
Beinn a'Chaorainn
Ben Avon
LAIRIG GHRU
Braeriach
Ben Macdui
The Sneck
Beinn a'Bhuird
Garbh Choire
Scor an
Lochain Uaine
Cairn Toul
GLEN DERRY
GLEN QUOICH
Corrour
The Devil's Point
GLEN LUIBEG
Derry Lodge
Linn of Dee

Heading up Glen Quoich

Just over the ford there is a track coming in from the right. Take this along the north side of the Quoich Water, passing through open Scots pine woodland. The track here runs roughly eastwards, and beyond the woodland it gets a bit vague. Cross to the south side of the river at a ford, and continue north-eastwards for two kilometres.

Then, where the valley turns northwards, climb uphill to the east to reach a major track below the west side of Meall an t-Slugain. Turn left along this track, heading northwards up towards the head of Glen Quoich. Here the Quoich Water should be to your left throughout as you head northwards towards the col known as The Sneck. You'll pass a prominent boulder – **Clach a'Chleirich** (The Cleric's Stone), and beyond this the valley closes in as you head just east of north towards the col at **The Sneck** (GR: NJ118010). You'll soon be wanting to think about where to camp for the night, and as you'll be returning to The Sneck after climbing **Ben Avon** to the east, you could camp here at the head of Glen Quoich, then leave all your heavy gear behind while you nip up to the summit.

From The Sneck climb stony slopes eastwards, keeping the cliffs of the **Garbh Choire** close by to your left throughout. Go over one broad bump on the Ben Avon plateau, then continue north-eastwards to the summit (GR: NJ133018), a granite tor at 1171m giving an easy scramble to the top. The summit itself is known as Leabaidh an Daimh Bhuidhe – the entire mountain goes under the name of Ben Avon. Return to The Sneck via the same route.

DAY 2

From The Sneck the ascent to your first Munro of the day, **Beinn a'Bhuird**, is easy. Climb westwards to the summit of the minor top known as **Cnap a'Chleirich**, then head just south of west to the summit of Beinn a'Bhuird (GR: NJ093006). This is marked by a small cairn at 1197m.

There's a huge expanse of featureless plateau to the west that needs to be crossed to gain access to the main Cairngorm massif, so this is a good point to consider if the weather conditions are suitable to continue.

If all is well, follow a compass bearing down to the very broad col at 831m (GR: NJ064003), then climb north-westwards for 2.2km to the summit of **Beinn a'Chaorainn** at 1083m (GR: NJ045014).

Walk northwards down from the summit, then veer north-west down to the **Fords of Avon** (GR: NJ042031).

Here you must cross the river. This can be dangerous when in spate, so consider carefully if it is safe for you to cross. Remember it may be wiser to wait for the water level to drop rather than attempt the river crossing in dangerous conditions – consider camping overnight if need be.

The Fords of Avon Refuge lies on the north side of the river, and from there you should turn westwards, following a path along the north bank until you reach **Loch Avon**, hemmed in by the rocky flanks of the Cairngorms.

Loch Avon from below The Saddle

Find a suitable campsite here for the night.

If you have energy to spare you could leave your heavy gear in camp and make an evening ascent of either **Bynack More** to the north, or **Beinn Mheadhoin** to the south. Both of these Munros are superb, and have fine granite tors scattered around their tops.

DAY 3

From the foot of Loch Avon (pronounced Aan), paths head round the loch on both sides. On the north-eastern tip of the loch there is a path junction. One path goes south-westwards along the north shore, while another climbs up to the west. To get to the summit of **Cairngorm**, you need to take this latter path. It climbs steadily to The Saddle, a windy col between Cairngorm and Bynack More.

If you're really keen to bag as many Munros as you can during this trip you could head north-east from The Saddle to climb Bynack More, but it is a long way out, and you'd have to go there and back.

To continue with the main route, follow a compass bearing north-west from the Saddle, aiming for the summit of Cairngorm at 1245m (GR: NJ005040). ▶

The name 'Cairngorm' confuses many people. 'Cairn' is Gaelic for 'stones' and 'gorm' translates as 'blue'. However, the granite of the Cairngorms appears red in colour. So, where does the name 'blue stones' originate? There is a gemstone found within the granite that is blue, and there are stories of 'cairngorm stone hunters' heading up onto the plateau in search of these. It is these blue stones that gave the massif the name, not the overall appearance of the range. Interestingly enough, the old name for the massif was Am Monadh Ruadh, which translates as 'The Red Hills'.

Head west from the summit and you'll pick up a path leading down to a large cairn at 1141m. South of here the ridge is rocky and has the cliffs of **Coire an t-Sneachda** to the north-west. Keep the top of these cliffs to your right and handrail around to the summit of Stob Coire an t-Sneachda at 1176m. Drop down just south of west to a stony col at the very head of Coire an t-Sneachda.

Cairngorm's summit is marked by a small automated weather station, with the summit cairn just to the north.

The weather station on the summit of Cairngorm

Now climb westwards, following the cliffs of Coire an Lochain to the summit of **Cairn Lochan** at 1215m.

Southwards the plateau opens up towards **Ben Macdui**, Britain's second highest mountain, and you should drop down to the broad col at the head of the **March Burn**. From here a bouldery path leads south-eastwards to the top of Ben Macdui at 1309m (GR: NN989989).

The route now lies to the west, and to gain the next range of hills – the **Braeriach** plateau – you'll need to descend all the way into the huge valley that lies in-between – the **Lairig Ghru**.

Head north-west from the summit of Ben Macdui, picking up a ridge above the burn of the Allt a'Choire Mhoir.

There's a lot of aircraft wreckage scattered around on this ridge, along with a memorial. This is the sad remains of a British services plane that crashed here in the 1940s.

Descend steep slopes to the west alongside the burn, into the Lairig Ghru. The way is rough, with lots of scree, but if you take it carefully this is an easy way down.

You should hit the Lairig Ghru path at a point where it leaves the side of the infant River Dee and cuts diagonally across the slopes to the south-east.

From this point cross the river, then contour around to the west on roughly the 680m contour. This will lead you into the **Garbh Choire** of Braeriach where you can either camp for the night, or make use of the primitive stone shelter marked on the OS maps as a bothy. This will put you in a good position for a long day tomorrow.

DAY 4

Start the day with a long and steep climb up onto the Braeriach plateau. If you head for the east side of **Coire Bhrochain** you will gain the plateau on the ridge between Sron na Lairig and the summit of Braeriach

Cairngorm from the top of the Goat Track

(GR: NN962999). Another option is to go north-west up the spur to the west of Coire Bhrochain, and so to the summit from there.

Braeriach's top lies at 1296m, right on the edge of the cliffs overlooking Coire Bhrochain (GR: NN953999). From the top, skirt around the head of a big gully cutting into the plateau to the south-west, then head south-west across the plateau to the rim of cliffs overlooking Garbh Choire. Follow this line of cliffs, handrailing around the corrie rim to the south and west, until you reach the broad flat top of **Carn na Criche** at 1265m.

Across the corrie to the south-east the lovely cone of **Sgor an Lochain Uaine** (GR: NN954976), or Angel's Peak, rises atop a scattering of slabs and boulders. To get to the summit you need to continue around the rim of the plateau keeping the cliffs of Garbh Choire Mor close by as a guide all the way.

Sgor an Lochain Uaine is a fabulous peak, and its summit at 1258m is a great place to relax and enjoy the views back across the corrie to Braeraich.

Slightly higher than Sgor an Lochain Uaine is **Cairn Toul** (GR: NN963972), lying a short way off to the south-east. Drop down into the col between the two, then climb easily up to the summit at 1291m.

Follow the ridge southwards off Cairn Toul, dropping first to a col, then climbing over a minor top, Stob Coire an t-Saighdeir at 1213m. Head south-east from its summit into a boggy col from where a path leads down Coire Odhar to the east to the bothy at **Corrour**.

Before dropping down from the col, consider whether you should climb **The Devil's Point** – Bod an Deamhain – the final Munro on this traverse, and only a short distance to the south-east. It only involves 100m of climbing, but you'll have to retrace your steps to the col to drop down into the Lairig Ghru.

Once down at Corrour bothy cross the river via the footbridge to the south-east and continue in the same direction at the path junction. Your route climbs gently around the flanks of **Carn a'Mhaim**, then takes you eastwards into the head of **Glen Luibeg**. Follow the path down the glen, keeping the river to your right until you reach the bridge at Derry Lodge (GR: NO040935). Cross the bridge and take the main track heading south-east alongside the Lui Water.

On your left you'll pass the path you climbed up on the first morning of your trip, then a little further on you should look out for the bridge over the river on the right. This leads back to the car park at the Linn of Dee, and the end of a very fine few days in Scotland's wildest mountains.

ROUTE 8
The Glen Muick High Level Circuit

Total Distance	32km
Daily Distances	Day 1 – 16km, Day 2 – 16km
Maps	Harvey British Mountain Map 1:40,000 (Cairngorms & Lochnagar)
Starting Point	Spittal of Glenmuick Car Park (GR: NO309851), south-west of Ballater

Area Summary

Lochnagar and its surrounding peaks really belong to the Cairngorms. They are a massive area of granite mountains, crag girt on many sides, and with superb tors crowning their summits. The area lies south of Deeside, backing on to the Balmoral Estate. Access is usually via Glen Muick, although the range can also be explored from Glen Esk, Glen Clova, or Glen Prosen in the south, or via Glen Callater, and also the Cairnwell Munros in the west.

Route Summary

A wonderfully wild traverse of this stunning valley. The route takes in all the Munros and Corbetts that ring the head of Glen Muick, starting with lowly Conachcraig, then taking in Lochnagar itself before finishing on Broad Cairn. This is a wild route on otherwise popular hills.

Tourist Information

There is a seasonal TIC in Ballater (tel 01339 741600) or you can call Braemar TIC (tel 01339 741600).

Accommodation and Supplies
In Ballater try the campsite on Anderson Road (tel 01339 755727). There are more options in Braemar. The Youth Hostels at Braemar (tel 01339 741659) is a good place to stay (website www.syha.org.uk).

Overnight Options
The best place to start looking for a wild campsite are around Carn a'Choire Bhoidheach and Carn an t-Sagairt Mor, although the possibilities are endless.

Escape Routes
Heading into the head of Glen Muick is the best option, but be aware that this is not possible from all points along the route. The vast crags of Eagles Rock (GR: NO235835) and Creag an Dubh-loch (GR: NO234823) should be avoided.

DAY 1
Start by heading north-west across the meadows below **Loch Muick**. There is a track across this way, that takes you over the River Muick to the **cottages** at Allt na Guibhsaich. There is a junction here, with the main track going straight ahead on its way towards Lochnagar. You can take this and miss out the Corbett of **Conachcraig**, but that would be a bit of a shame as it's a lovely hill and gives superb views into the north-east corrie of Lochnagar from its summit.

Turn right at Allt na Guibhsaich, walking beneath a stand of ancient Scots pines, and continue for 1km to another junction. Take the path to the left, slanting gently up the hillside to the north. As the path comes around into the little valley holding the Allt Vitch you should break out of the forest plantation you are in, walking off the path on a bearing south-westward to gain the east ridge of Conachcraig. Climb around the rocky spur of Carn an Daimh, passing the small crags to your right, then continue up the broad slopes to the summit of Conachcraig at 865m (GR: NO279865).

To the south-west there is a col at 697m, which connects Conachcraig with Lochnagar. Drop down to this

Route 8:
The Glen Muick High Level Circuit

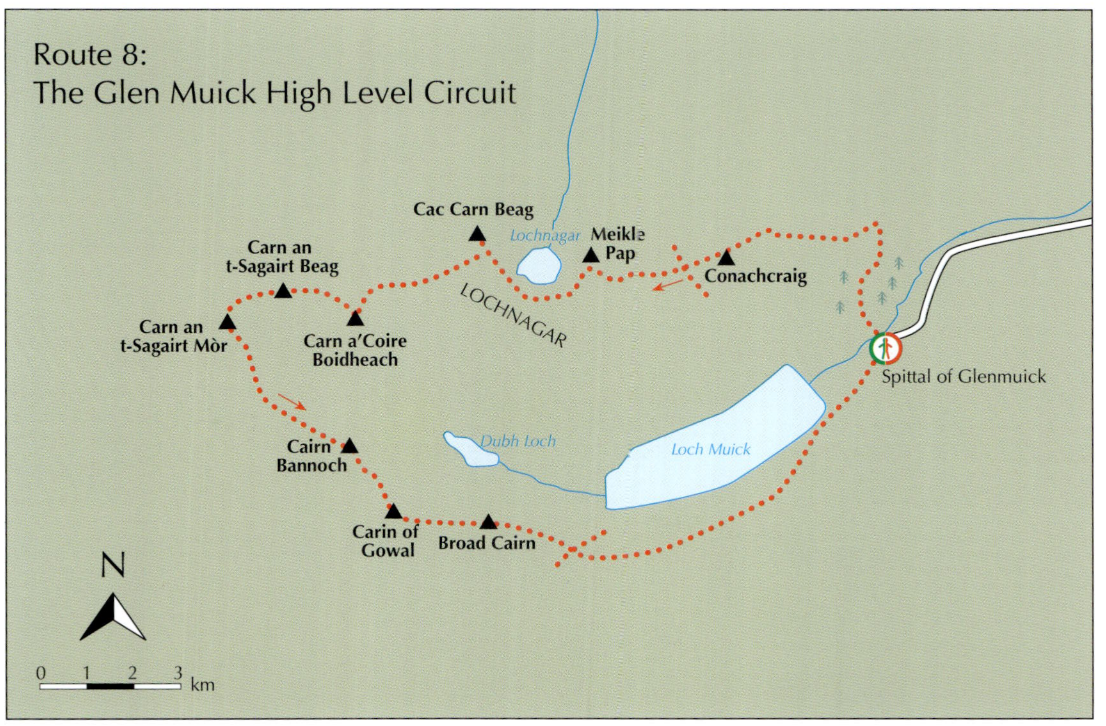

The views to your right are incredible, with the vast amphitheatre of the Corrie of **Lochnagar** thrusting rocky arêtes from the lake, Lochnagar, that gives the mountain its name.

col, then pick up the path westwards towards the stony corrie below **Meikle Pap**. This is the little knoll on the north-eastern ridge of Lochnagar's summit plateau. Where this knoll adjoins into the plateau, at a col (GR: NO258858) the path turns sharp left, climbing steeply onto the main plateau. ◄

Climb southwards onto the plateau, reaching it at the spot height at 1078m, just north-west of **Cuidhe Crom**. Keep the crag edge close by to your right, handrailing around its rim to the vast cairn at Cac Carn Mor, which at 1150m is actually not the highest point of Lochnagar. The summit, Cac Carn Beag, at 1155m, lies 500m northwards across the plateau, and it is an easy walk to the granite tor with its OS trig pillar (GR: NO244861).

Leave the summit and walk to the south-west, following the edge of Coire **Loch nan Eun** until you are high above the loch itself deep in the corrie to your right.

From here you can walk easily south-westwards to the top of your second Munro, **Carn a'Coire Boidheach** at 1110m (GR: NO227845).

The plateau here and further west towards **Carn an t-Sagairt Mòr** rolls gently and is mainly grassy, making for a number of good camping spots.

DAY 2

To the north-west of Carn a'Choire Bhoidheach there is a small subsidiary peak known as **Carn an t-Sagairt Beag**, and you should traverse its top before heading down to the grassy col between it and **Carn an t-Sagairt Mòr**. The top of this latter peak has the sad remains of a crashed aircraft on its summit plateau.

From the cairn on the summit at 1047m (GR: NO207844) a path heads south-east and you should follow this over grassy ground, dropping to the very broad and rough col between Carn an t-Sagairt Mor and **Cairn Bannoch**. Continue south-eastwards to the big summit cairn on Cairn Bannoch's summit at 1012m (GR: NO 223825). The broad ridge continues south-eastwards over **Cairn of Gowal** at 991m, then down to a col above the impressive crags of **Creag an Dubh-loch**. You can wander

Lochnagar

northwards to the top of the crag's south-east buttress for spectacular views down into the corrie that holds the wonderfully remote **Dubh Loch**.

To the south-east lies the top of the final Munro of the trip, **Broad Cairn**. An easy ascent over grass then rough granite boulders leads to its summit cairn at 998m (GR: NO240815).

Descend eastwards along the path over Little Craig, and then turn south-eastwards into a col. A major track cuts over the col here from the head of Glen Clova to Corrie Chash at the head of Loch Muick, and you can descend this track to the east, following the track along the south side of Loch Muick back to the car park.

If you want to stay on the tops a bit longer, you could climb south-eastwards to the summit of **Sandy Hillock** at 768m (GR: NO266804), then follow the broad and heathery ridge south-eastwards over Broom Hill to Dog Hillock (GR: NO286794). From the flat top of Dog Hillock descend eastwards to pick

Backpacking on Lochnagar in Winter

up the Capel Road – an ancient track cutting over the hills. Turn northwards along the track, following it over an undulating moorland to a descent to the eastern end of Loch Muick. Turn right once on the track through the glen and you'll soon be back to the car park.

ROUTE 9

Glen Lee and Glen Mark

Total Distance	40km
Daily Distances	Day 1 – 19km, Day 2 – 21km
Maps	OS Landranger sheet 44 (Ballater)
Starting Point	Car park at the head of Glen Esk (GR: NO 447804)

Area Summary

This wild and remote area south-east of Lochnagar and
Glen Muick is little visited by walkers. Only the Munro,
Mount Keen, sees its fair share of visitors, and even that
hill is scorned by many. The general scenery here is open
moorland and blanket bog, while the glens that cut into
these hills are wild and beautiful. This is an explorer's
paradise, and once you've been bitten by the bug, you'll
want to return here time and time again.

Route Summary

A round of the high moors circling the head of Glen Esk,
where it splits into two – Glen Mark and Glen Lee. The
route takes in the Munro, Mount Keen, as well as a number of other, lesser summits, including Fasheilach, Green
Hill, and Ben Tirran. The outward journey is made via
Glen Mark, while the return brings you down to the
southern shores of Loch Lee.

Tourist Information

There is a Tourist Information Centre at Brechin Castle Centre, in Brechin (tel
01356 623050) www.angusanddundee.co.uk.

Accommodation and Supplies

Brechin is the nearest place accommodation and supplies, and there are plenty of options there. For accommodation information call the TIC (above).

Overnight Options

The Mountain Bothies Association maintains a bothy at Shielin of Mark (GR: NO337827), which is at roughly the halfway point. There are lots of good places to camp too in these gentle hills.

Escape Routes

It is possible to descend alongside the Water of Mark on its north side, although this does involve a couple of minor river crossings. The track up Glen Lee is useful too, and runs right up onto the moors to a point very close to the Shielin of Mark Bothy.

DAY 1

Start the walk by heading along the road from the car park a short way, until you reach a junction near the bridge over the **Water of Mark**. Ignore the road going over the bridge, and instead go north-eastwards up the east side of Glen Mark. The track here is easy to follow, and takes you all the way up into the heart of this wild glen. After 4km you'll reach the **Queen's Well**.

The Queen's Well was built in commemoration of Queen Victoria who once stopped here for a drink of water on her way from Deeside to Glenesk. It is thought likely that she was accompanied by the famed John Brown during this visit.

Just beyond the well there is a track junction, and here you should take the track to the right, passing by the farm at Glenmark as you begin the climb towards **Mount Keen**. The track follows the Ladder Burn, to the right of the rocky ridge of Couternach, and then emerges onto the moorland plateau at the Knowe of Crippley. Here there is another track junction – one track heads north-

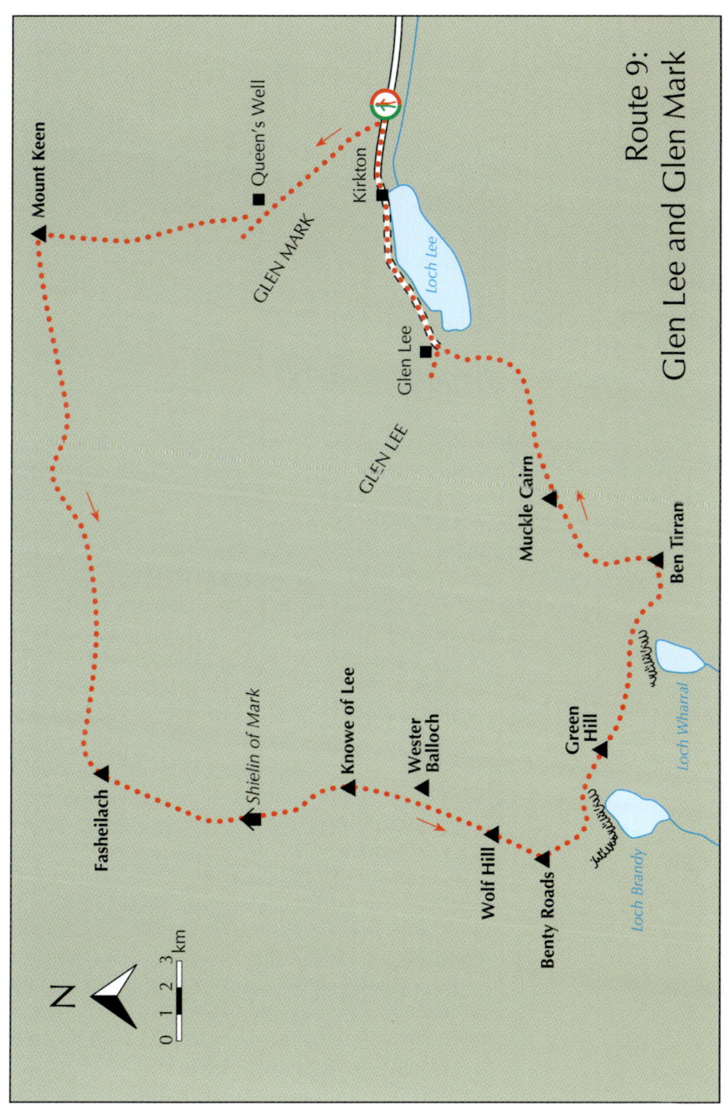
Mount Keen
Queen's Well
Kirkton
GLEN MARK
Loch Lee
Glen Lee
GLEN LEE
Muckle Cairn
Ben Tirran
Loch Wharral
Fasheilach
Shielin of Mark
Knowe of Lee
Wester Balloch
Green Hill
Wolf Hill
Benty Roads
Loch Brandy
Route 9:
Glen Lee and Glen Mark
N
0 1 2 3 km

The Queen's Well in Glen Mark

Mount Keen is the easternmost of all the Munros.

wards, bypassing the summit cone of Mount Keen, while the other branches off to the right and makes directly for the summit.

The going to the summit is easy, and the top is soon reached at 939m (GR: NO409869). ◄

From the summit the route now takes you over many a pathless and rough moorland mile. Turn westwards and descend the steep slopes, crossing the track that bypassed the summit to the west. Make towards the little hill known as the Head of Black Bush (746m), then take a bearing to the south-west across the barren moors to a group of small lochans (GR: NO390865). There is a very broad ridge running north-westwards and you should follow this for 1.5km, following the county boundary line and continuing alongside of this as it swings to the south-west towards a spot height (664m) above the **Burn of Fasheilach** (GR: NO363863). Ahead now, to the west, the small rise of **Fasheilach** itself can be seen. Follow a bearing over the rough moorland making for the summit trig pillar at 721m (GR: NO342858).

The county boundary now swings away to the south, and then back to the west to another spot height at 698m (GR: NO335849), although you don't have to follow the exact line of the boundary (there is no fence, or even posts to mark this anyway).

From the 698m spot height it is just over 2km directly to the bothy at **Shielin of Mark** – you should aim pretty much straight for it as this line will keep you on the highest ground, passing close by a small lochan on the left.

DAY 2

Heathery slopes rise to the south of the bothy at Shielin of Mark, first to the **Round Hill of Mark**, then onwards to **Gowan Knowe**. Start by crossing the burn outside the bothy (this is the headwaters of the Water of Mark) then climb steadily up the easy-angled slopes, veering slightly to the south-east from the Round Hill of Mark to gain Gowan Knowe. Continue in the same direction, climbing still until you get to the top of the little knoll known as the **Knowe of Lee** (GR: NO342803).

To the south-west there is a col separating Knowe of Lee from the next hill, **Wester Balloch**, and you should drop down to this col then climb southwards. The summit of Wester Balloch is fairly undistinguished at 806m (GR: NO 342790), but better things await you to the south.

Descend south-westwards to cross the Water of Unich, then climb steeply out of the trench to the top of Wolf Hill, continuing to the wonderfully named Benty Roads at 841m (GR: NO331766).

Less than 1km to the south, the flanks of the hill fall dramatically into the depths of the lovely wooded **Glen Clova**, and the next section of the walk is perhaps the most spectacular on this route.

Descend from Benty Roads to the south, down to a col between the Burn of Longshank to the north-east, and the Corrie Burn which gushes down the Corrie of Clova to the south-west. Walk southwards from the col, climbing to the ragged edge known as the Snub to get magnificent views right down into Glen Clova, and more intimate glimpses of the Corrie of Clova closer at hand to the west. ▶ To get to Green Hill simply skirt around the head of the corrie holding Loch Brandy, following a path all the way and climbing gently to the summit at 870m (GR: NO348756).

Down in the deep hanging valley immediately east of the Snub lies **Loch Brandy**, with the lovely little **Green Hill** rising on the other side.

Looking up to the head of Glen Mark

The path continues to the south-east for 400m, then splits. Ignore both ways and instead continue to the south-east to the top of the cliffs at Craigs of Loch Wharral, which fall from beneath your feet down to the hidden loch of the same name. Skirt around the top edge of the crags, handrailing as you go until you can branch out to the east to the summit of **Ben Tirran**, known as the Goet at 896m (GR: NO374746).

Northwards from the Goet it is 1.5km down to pick up a track over **Muckle Cairn**. This track goes north-eastwards, passing East Cairn, then just to the north of the spur of **Wester Skuiley**. The path brings you out at the lip of a deep and steep-sided valley overlooking the wonderfully-named **Shank of Inchgrundle**, then takes you down this hill. Ignore a path going off to the right at a stream. You'll soon find yourself at Inchgrundle itself, just above **Loch Lee**. Drop down through the woods of Inchgrundle, then follow the track out to cross the Water of Lee at the bridge where it flows into Loch Lee. Over the bridge turn right and follow the track on the north shore of the loch, passing **Kirkton** on your way back to your car.

ROUTE 10

Mount Battock and Clachnaben from Glen Esk

Total Distance	33km
Daily Distances	Day 1 – 21km, Day 2 – 12km
Maps	OS Landranger sheets 44 (Ballater) & 45 (Stonehaven & Banchory)
Starting Point	Park sensibly at Millden Lodge in Glen Esk (GR: NO541789)

Area Summary

This wild area of grouse moors, offering a good network of paths and tracks onto the tops, is a superb place to get away from it all for a couple of days. The area is sandwiched between Royal Deeside to the north, and the coastal arable lands of Strathmore to the south. There is a road (the B974) cutting over the range to the east, which gives good access, while other approaches are long and arduous.

Route Summary

This is a shorter route than most of the others in this guide, and is ideal for those new to the delights of backpacking. This route takes in the wild moors around Glen Dye from a starting point in Glen Esk. The remote Corbett of Mount Battock is climbed on the first day before a traverse eastwards over the moors to the tor-topped hill of Clachnaben. A night in the comfortable House of Charr bothy, or a camp by the river is followed by a route back over the hills from the head of Glen Dye.

DAY 1

From the road up Glen Esk take the minor lane which branches off to the north immediately west of the bridge over the **Burn of Turret**. This lane goes to Mill of Aucheen, and just beyond the mill you should turn right

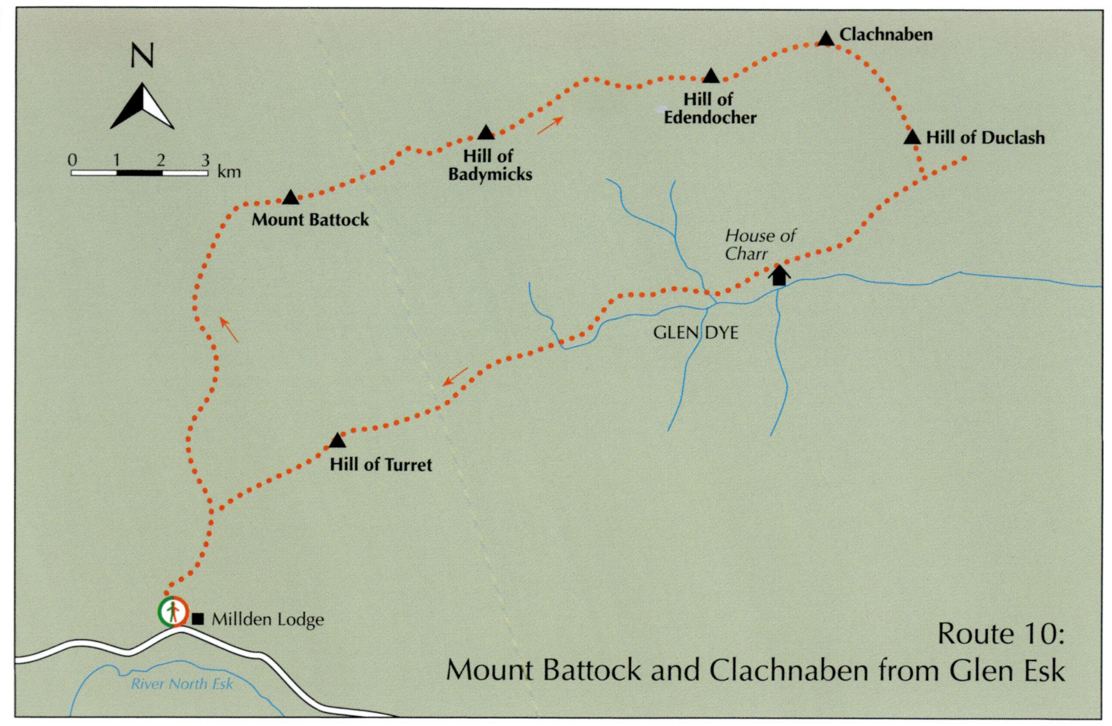
N
0   1   2   3   km
Clachnaben
Hill of Edendocher
Hill of Badymicks
Hill of Duclash
Mount Battock
House of Charr
GLEN DYE
Hill of Turret
Millden Lodge
River North Esk
Route 10:
Mount Battock and Clachnaben from Glen Esk

Tourist Information
There is a TIC on Bridge Street in Banchory (tel 01330 822000), while the one at Brechin Castle Centre, in Brechin (tel 01356 623050) is also very useful.

Accommodation and Supplies
Banchory is the nearest place to the north for accommodation and supplies, while Brechin lies to the south and also has lots of options.

Overnight Options
The Mountain Bothies Association maintains a bothy known as House of Charr, which lies in Glen Dye (GR: NO616831). There are plenty of good places to camp too alongside the river in Glen Dye.

Escape Routes
There is a good network of tracks running across these hills from Glen Esk to Glen Dye, and any of these would make suitable escape routes. Bear in mind, though, that in an emergency both glens are still remote, and help could be a long way down (or up!) either glen.

and follow a track that heads back towards the burn. Go over a side stream, then take the left fork at a junction in the track – don't cross over the Burn of Turret. The track goes north-west, and then curves around to the north-east around the little hill of **Allrey**. To the east of Allrey the track crosses the head of the Burn of Turret at the confluence of the side streams, the White Burn and the Black Burn (GR: NO543826).

Once over the stream the track soon fizzles out on the western slopes of **Mount Battock**, and you should first aim for a prominent cairn on the knoll to the west of the summit. Then turn eastwards and follow the easy ground to the summit of Mount Battock at 778m (GR: NO549845). ▶

Mount Battock is the most easterly Corbett, and is also the highest hill in the eastern Mounth. The views from the summit are extensive.

The Mounth is a huge area of the Grampians generally regarded as being everything east of the Cairnwell Pass

Clachnaben from Glen Esk

and Glenshee. It includes Lochnagar itself, and rolls away eastwards towards Stonehaven on the coast.

Eastwards towards the rocky tor of **Clachnaben** there is a series of bull-dozed landrover tracks across the moor that make for easy walking. Leave Mount Battock by heading just north of east to pick up a track near a hut (GR: NO566849). Follow the track eastwards, ignoring the track off to the right at a junction 1.2km from the hut.

Continue over **Hill of Badymicks**, then onwards to **Sandy Hill**, staying on the track the whole time.

You'll soon reach the **Hill of Edendocher** (GR: NO604859) where the track swings away to the south. To the east, Clachnaben now dominates the view. There is an electric deer fence running along the ridge here, and other fences come up out of the glens. There are stiles at the crossing points, and you'll soon find yourself on the magnificent 30m high granite tors of Clachnaben's summit at 589m (GR: NO614865).

The local spelling of the name is Clochna'bain, and it comes from the Gaelic Clach na Beinne, which means simply 'stone of the hill'.

Descend south-eastwards to the **Hill of Duclash**, then south over Nettle Hill to a track running along the flanks of the hill overlooking **Glen Dye**. Turn right here, westwards, and walk up the glen. Cross the Burn of Waterhead, and then continue for 1.5km to the stone bothy at Charr, known as the **House of Charr**.

DAY 2

After a good night's sleep in the House of Charr walk westwards along the track up the glen. Continue to where the valley splits, the stream on the right being the Burn of Badymicks, while the Water of Dye comes down from the west on the left. Cross the Burn of Badymicks and take the track up alongside the Water of Dye, keeping to its north side until the track peters out. Continue on a very vague path through the heather, heading south-westwards to the crest of the hill which is just to the west of **Hill of Fingray** (GR: NO562817). There's a new electric deer fence here, and you should cross over this and head down to the south-west, crossing the head of the Burn of Leuchary to pick up a track on the **Hill of Turret**. Turn downhill and follow this track westwards down to the **Burn of Turret**. Cross the burn and turn left, down the same track you took on the way out yesterday morning.

The Charr Bothy in Glen Dye

ROUTE 11

Jock's Road and Tolmount

Total Distance	42km
Daily Distances	Day 1 – 27km, Day 2 – 15km
Maps	OS Landranger sheets 43 (Braemar) & 44 (Ballater)
Starting Point	Car park at the head of Glen Doll (GR: NO284761)

Area Summary

The Angus Glens are a world away from the rest of the Grampians. Glen Clova itself is one of the most important valleys running out to the North Sea to the southeast of these hills. It is a wild area of moorland hills falling to deep valleys with very rough and craggy flanks.

Route Summary

The route starts with a wonderfully wild high-level traverse of the Munros on the west side of Glen Glova, over Driesh and Mayar, then northwards to the Tolmount. Carn of Claise and Carn an Tuirc are crossed before a good track is followed down into Glen Callater. The old track known as Jock's Road is taken on the second day, cutting across the hills via a high pass, then down into the head of Glen Doll.

Tourist Information

There is a Tourist Information Centre on Castle Street in Dundee (tel 01382 572572, website www.angusanddundee.co.uk).

Accommodation and Supplies

Sadly, the campsite and the SYHA Hostel shown on the OS map as being at the head of Glen Doll have both closed. However, the Clova Hotel just down the glen is superb and offers accommodation in the hotel, self-catering

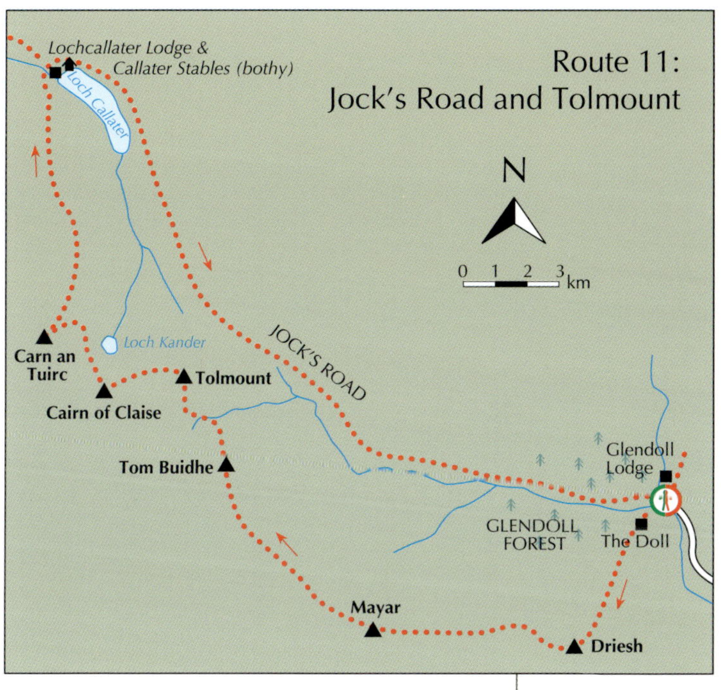

lodges, or a bunkhouse (tel 015757 550350, website www.clova.com). The nearest town for shops is Kirriemuir, further down the glen.

Overnight Options

There is an open bothy at Callater Stables, next to Lochcallater Lodge at the north-western end of Loch Callater (GR: NO178844), or you could camp at the head of the loch in Glen Callater.

Escape Routes

Jock's Road is the easiest way through these mountains, and should be followed in an emergency. From the Tolmount and other Munros to the west of Jock's Road it is possible to descend westwards to Cairnwell Pass road which leads northwards to Braemar.

DAY 1

From the car park in Glen Doll (pronounced Dole) go westwards for a short way towards **Glendoll Lodge**, then take the bridge on the left over White Water. Follow the track to the cottage known as **The Doll**, then skirt around the forest edge to the foot of the steep but brilliant ridge known as **The Scorrie**. Climb this fantastic rocky crest, high above **Corrie Winter** (wrongly named the Winter Corrie on the OS Landranger), to the summit of **Driesh** at 947m (GR: NO272736). The summit of this Munro is marked by an OS trig pillar, and a fence that runs westwards towards your next objective, **Mayar**.

Follow the fence down to an obvious col at the head of the Burn of Kilbo, then continue westwards alongside the fence to the second Munro, Mayar at 928m (GR: NO241738).

Leave the summit of Mayar and walk north-westwards to the top of **Dun Hillocks** at 890m. ◀ Skirt around the corrie rim to the north, then leave its edge to continue northwards to the summit of **Tom Buidhe** at 957m, the third Munro of the day (GR: NO213787).

The next summit, Tolmount, lies just over a kilometre away to the north, but to get there it is easier to first head just north of west to the head of a burn, then turn north-east up easy slopes to the summit at 958m (GR: NO210800).

That's four Munros so far, and two more await before you'll head down into the depths of Glen Callater.

Almost 3km away to the south-west, the highest hill of the six you'll traverse today rises in stony slopes, and it is an easy walk across the plateau to this Munro, **Carn of Claise** at 1064m (GR: NO185789).

A path passes over the summit of Carn of Claise, heading roughly northwards, and you should follow this, curving off to the north-west to climb the final peak of the day, **Carn an Tuirc** at 1019m (GR: NO173804). Head eastwards along the summit ridge, dropping slightly as you approach the head of the **Loch Kander** corrie. Here you'll pick up the path again, and you can follow this, initially around the rim of the corrie, then north-westwards

Walking on the Tolmount Munros

down the long heathery flanks of the north-east ridge of Carn an Tuirc. The path becomes more obvious, and takes you all the way down to the Callater Stables, where you can spend the night.

DAY 2

To the south-east of Callater Stables **Loch Callater** stretches away towards the head of the glen, and paths run along either shore. Personally, I prefer the one on the north side, but it really doesn't matter which path you choose. From the head of the loch the path keeps to the north side of the burn, the Allt an Loch, and climbs steeply up the valley headwall to the top of the pass taken by Jock's Road.

Jock's Road is probably an old drove road, and claims to be one of the first Scottish Rights of Way. The owner of the Glen Doll Estate in the late 19th century, Duncan Macpherson, tried to ban access to his land, including the use of Jock's road through his estate. He

Loch Callater in winter

was challenged by the Scottish Rights of Way Society, and some say the action was initiated by a certain John Winters, after whom Jock's Road was named. After a long and expensive court battle the society won their case, and Jock's Road was made a right of way, but only after both the society and Macpherson had been made bankrupt.

The top of the pass is at 883m (GR: NO218804), and just beyond this point to the south the path actually follows a ridge for a while, climbing higher than the pass. It passes to the east of **Crow Craigies**, reaching 910m, then drops to a flatter area before veering off into the head of Glen Doll below **Cairn Lunkard**.

Throughout the descent the path keeps to the east side of the White Water, entering the dense forests of Glen Doll before curving around to the east as it brings you to the car park near Glendoll Lodge.

ROUTE 12

The Glenshee Munros

Total Distance	40km
Daily Distances	Day 1 – 19km, Day 2 – 21km
Maps	Harvey British Mountain Map 1:40,000 (Cairngorms & Lochnagar)
Starting Point	Spittal of Glenshee car park (GR: NO108701), just off the A93 between Braemar and Blairgowrie

Area Summary

The wild hills to the west of the Glenshee skiing area. Although the hills overlooking the A93 (the Cairnwell and Cairn Aosda) suffer from being covered in ski tows, the rest of this range is wild and has a very remote feeling to it. There are lots of options for backpacking here. This route takes in some of the Munros of the region, but there are others you can include if the fancy takes you.

Route Summary

The route goes up Glen Lochsie from the Spittal of Glenshee, first heading for Glas Tulaichean. It then takes you northwards into the wild country around Loch nan Eun where you could set up camp for the night, then nip out, unencumbered by your heavy pack, to climb a number of Munros. The route then takes you east to the Cairnwell Munros, before descending the south ridge of Carn a'Gheoidh to the Corbett of Ben Gulabin. The Spittal of Glenshee lies just south of this hill.

Tourist Information
There is a TIC in Braemar TIC (tel 01339 741600).

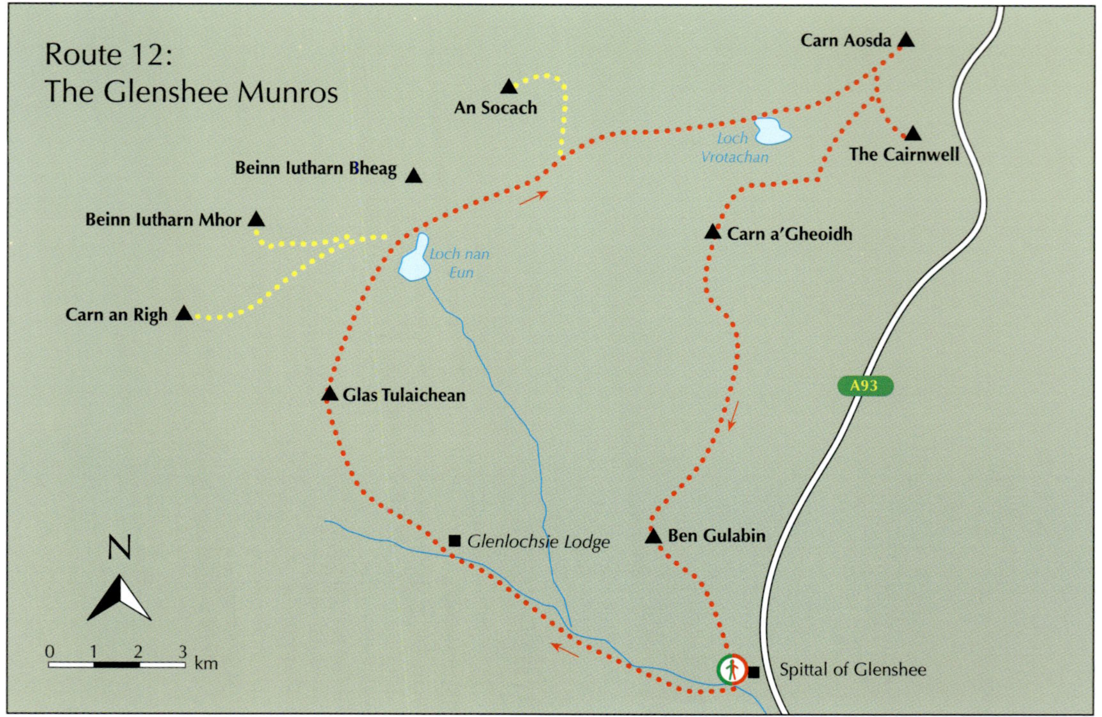

Route 12:
The Glenshee Munros
Carn Aosda
An Socach
Loch Vrotachan
The Cairnwell
Beinn Iutharn Bheag
Beinn Iutharn Mhor
Carn a'Gheoidh
Loch nan Eun
Carn an Righ
A93
Glas Tulaichean
Glenlochsie Lodge
Ben Gulabin
N
0 1 2 3 km
Spittal of Glenshee

Accommodation and Supplies
There are lots of good options in Braemar. The Youth Hostel (tel 01339 741659) is a good place to stay (website www.syha.org.uk). There's also the hotel and bunkhouse at the Spittal of Glenshee (tel 01250 855215, www.spittalofglenshee.co.uk). You could also try the Dalmunzie Hotel (tel 01250 885224, www.dalmunzie.com), which lies just up the glen from Spittal.

Overnight Options
Camp wild somewhere in the vicinity of Loch nan Eun (GR: NO065783), or beneath the south face of An Sochach, a little further on.

Escape Routes
Make for either Gleann Taitneach, which leads south to Spittal of Glenshee, or head east for the Cairnwell Pass road (A93).

DAY 1
Begin on the south side of the river at **Spittal of Glenshee**. There are two tracks that head south-west up onto the hills – one goes up beside a burn into Coire Lairige, while the other heads towards the bottom corner of a small plantation. Take this latter track up to the plantation (GR: NO104697). Follow the track into the plantation, going north-westwards, then out at the other side onto the open hillside above the glen. Continue walking north-westwards to a second small plantation, and go through that too, descending slightly, then emerging onto a steep hillside. Follow the path down to the river.

The path continues north-westwards up the south side of the Glen Lochsie Burn, and you should follow it as far as **Glenlochsie Lodge** where it crosses the stream via a footbridge. Beyond the lodge the path continues north-westwards (this path is not shown on the OS Landranger map, but is marked on the Harvey British Mountain Map). The path climbs steeply up the ridge, keeping the Allt Clais Mhor to its right. Follow it onto the broad southern ridge of **Glas Tulaichean** – the ridge being marked on the map as Breac-reidh. Once on Breac-reidh turn northwards and follow the ridge, bearing slightly north-east as it narrows, to the summit of this fine Munro. Glas Tulaichean's top is marked by an OS trig pillar at 1051 (GR: NO052760).

The summit of Glas Tulaichean is quite complicated, having five ridges radiating from the central point. There is the long south ridge that you have just climbed, then a west ridge that leads out to Faire Ghlinne Mhoir. To the north-east the ridge splits just 400m from the top, with one branch going north and down to **Loch nan Eun**, while the other is narrow and falls steeply eastwards into **Gleann Taitneach**. The final ridge runs to the south-east, ending in Creag Bhreac above Glenlochsie Lodge (this ridge makes a fine alternative to the ascent route you've taken).

To continue, go north east from the summit to the junction of the northern and eastern ridge. Take the north ridge, high above Glas Choire Bheag, and down to a spot height at 933m.

At the spot height turn north-eastwards and drop down to a col, following a path all the way, then walk over a small knoll on the north-east side of the col and you will see Loch nan Eun dead ahead.

You could camp somewhere around Loch nan Eun, and this makes a great spot to leave your heavy backpacking gear so that you can head up onto the heights of the two Munros that rise to the west.

Beinn Iutharn Mhor (GR: NO046793) can be climbed by heading north-west from Loch nan Eun up to a col, then traversing west to a higher col between **Mam nan Carn** and Beinn Iutharn Mhor. A path leads up the south ridge of Beinn Iutharn Mhor to the summit at 1045m.

You can also use this route to climb **Carn an Righ** (GR: NO028773). From the col above Loch nan Eun climb south-westwards to the top of Mam nan Carn, then down to the col between it and Carn an Righ. The eastern flank of Carn an Righ is broad and has a vague path up to the summit at 1029m.

The key to the main backpacker's route is Loch nan Eun, and if you take on the challenge of these two Munros you should return to this point.

From Loch nan Eun head northwards along the burn that issues from the loch. Don't descend too far down into the head of the valley here though, as you need to be making for a high col over and above the eastern side of the valley head (GR: NO082794). This makes another good place to camp up for the night, and puts you in place to bag **An Socach** (GR: NO079799) immediately above to the north, before you get into your sleeping bag for the night.

An Socach is an easy climb to the north. Go up gentle slopes to gain the ridge to the east of the summit, then

Carn Aosda summit from across the Cairnwell Pass (Day 2)

*The summit of
The Cairnwell*

turn west to the top at 944m. Return to your tent via the same route.

DAY 2

From the col on the south side of An Socach begin the day by heading for the south-east side of the Baddoch Burn. Follow the burn for 2km, until it begins to swing away to the north-east and descends into the head of the glen, and from there take a bearing eastwards across the heathery hillside to **Loch Vrotachan** (GR: NO120785). Immediately above the loch to the north-east lies **Carn Aosda** at 917m (GR: NO133792) and a vague ridge leads easily up this peak. Climb above the loch and you will pick up a track that leads through all the skiing paraphernalia to the summit cairn.

Drop back down the same way to a col, then climb up to the south-east to the top of **The Cairnwell**, at 933m your second Munro of the day. The Cairnwell's top is also bristling with skiing detritus, including tows, fences, and a hut just off the summit cairn.

Turn your back to all this rubbish and head north-westwards back down towards the col between the Cairnwell and Carn Aosda. Just before you reach the col, on a little rocky knoll, you'll spot a path heading north-westwards around the head of Choire Dhirich which falls away to the south. Skirt around the corrie headwall, picking up a ridge that leads to **Carn nan Sac** at 920m. The ridge continues westwards to the summit of **Carn a'Gheoidh** at 975m (GR: NO107767), the final Munro of this trip.

It's not over yet though – you still have a long descent to make to get back to the Spittal of Glenshee.

Walk south-west downhill for 1km, then climb gently to the south-east to the summit of **Carn Mor**. The ridge now runs southwards to **Creagan Bheithe** at 759m (GR: NO109735), and you should follow it to the top of this mound. Now descend steeply to the south-west, dropping to a col below the steep flanks of **Ben Gulabin**. ▶ Climb steeply up the north-east flank, topping out at 806m (GR: NO101722). From the summit follow the ridge eastwards, curving around to the south-east for a steep descent to the old kirk in Spittal of Glenshee.

This is a fine little Corbett, and it is well worth ascending as a final fling before heading for the glen.

ROUTE 13
The Blair Atholl Munros

Total Distance	50km
Daily Distances	Day 1 – 24km, Day 2 – 26km
Maps	OS Landranger sheet 43 (Braemar & Blair Atholl)
Starting Point	Blair Atholl railway station (GR: NN870653).

Note The start of this route involves a short amount of road walking to get into the hills. If this really isn't your thing you could call the TIC in Pitlochry for the number of a local taxi company who will run you from Blair Atholl to the start of the track. You need to get to the end of the public road at Loch Moraig (GR: NN905671).

Area Summary

A fantastic area to the north and east of the A9 at Blair Atholl. These are the southern fringes of the Cairngorms range, and many of the mountains and glens here feel as remote as any you'd find within the range. The area is sliced in two by the impressive trench of Glen Tilt, and this in itself forms a superb through-route to Braemar (see Route 14).

Route Summary

The route takes in all the Munros that crowd around the trench of Glen Tilt, starting with the three summits of Beinn a'Ghlo. The route then takes you into Glen Tilt before ascending onto the wild hills north of the glen. Beinn Dearg is the final Munro of this trip, before you head south back to Blair Atholl.

DAY 1

Begin by leaving **Blair Atholl** on the lane towards the **Old Bridge of Tilt**, which branches off the B8079 just to

Tourist Information
The TIC in Pitlochry is great for advice on transport and accommodation. You'll find it on Atholl Road (tel 01796 472215).

Accommodation and Supplies
In Blair Atholl there is the Atholl Arms Hotel (tel 01796 481205), or for a cheaper option stay at the campsite at Blair Castle (tel 01796 481263). There are plenty of other options in Pitlochry – call the TIC for information.

Overnight Options
Camp wild either in Glen Tilt, or perhaps at the top of the zigzags above Forest Lodge near the Allt na Maraig (GR: NN933755).

Escape Routes
Glen Tilt is the obvious escape route. Head south-west down the glen to Blair Atholl (it's a very long way through to Braemar in the other direction!).

the east of the Bridge of Tilt. Follow the lane along the east side of the river to the Old Bridge, bearing right here, and then right again after 550m. The road goes steeply uphill to the east, and ends at **Loch Moraig**.

Beyond Loch Moraig a track heads north-east to an old bothy, now disused. Ahead the fine south-western ridge of **Carn Liath**, the first Munro on the round of **Beinn a'Ghlo**, rises above the surrounding moorland.

A path can be seen cutting across the heather towards this ridge, and you should follow it over the moor, scattering mountain hares and red grouse as you go. Although the ridge is steep the going is straightforward. You soon find yourself reaching the crest of the summit ridge, then it's just a short stroll northwards to the OS trig pillar of Carn Liath at 975m (GR: NN936698).

This is the first peak on the round of three Munros known collectively as Beinn a'Ghlo. To continue the traverse of the three head north-west down a narrow ridge from the summit of Carn Liath. The ridge bends around to the north, then curves all the way around to the

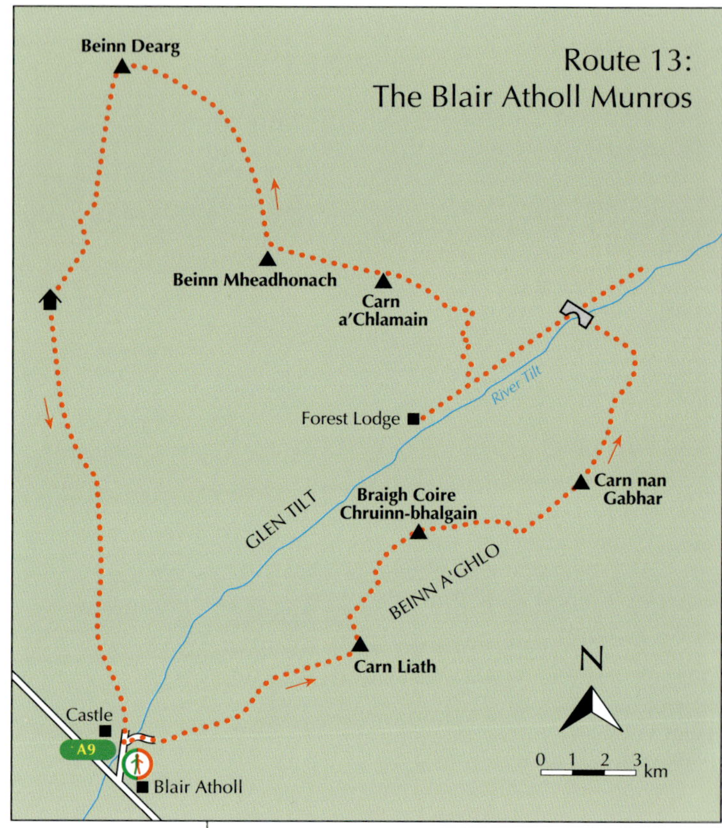

The summit cairn sits close to the edge of the drop into Glen Tilt and the views into the glen are impressive.

north-east to a minor top known as Beinn Mhaol. North again the way drops steeply to a col at the foot of the next Munro, **Braigh Coire Chruinn-bhalgain**. From the col, head eastwards initially, then curve around to the north after 500m and climb straight up the steep face to the summit at 1070m (GR: NN946724). ◄

Go north-east for 300m, then drop down slightly to the east to a col before a small bump on the ridge. Walk north-east again, over this bump, but do not continue

Beinn a'Ghlo range

along the main ridge as this descends straight down into **Glen Tilt**, and you'll miss the final and highest Munro of this group. From the south end of a high col, just over the bump on the ridge (GR: NN953728) follow a ridge steeply down to a col between Braigh Coire Chruinn-bhalgain and **Carn nan Gabhar**, the final peak of the Beinn a'Ghlo round. The climb up eastwards is steep and leads onto the summit ridge. Turn north-east to gain the summit at 1120m. An OS trig pillar marks the highest point (GR: NN971733).

The north ridge of Carn nan Gabhar is the key to getting down into Glen Tilt. It starts off heading just east of north, then takes you down a stony staircase to a col. Walk up and over a minor top on the ridge then down into another col before **Meall a'Mhuirich** at 898m. Go over Meall a'Mhuirich, and walk north-westwards down a broadening ridge until you can make for the **bridge** over the **River Tilt** near the foot of the Allt Fheannach (GR: NN956763).

Cross the bridge to the track that runs up the entire length of Glen Tilt. Turn left and follow the track down the glen, passing beneath the crags of Creag a'Chrochaidh,

Wild Camping above Glen Tilt

then along the bottom edge of a plantation. As you near a smaller plantation just before reaching **Forest Lodge** (GR: NN934743) you should look for a path cutting up the steep hillside to the north of the glen in a series of tight zigzags. Follow this path until the gradient eases at a knoll, and you can drop over the back of this knoll to find a campsite by the stream at **Allt na Maraig**.

DAY 2

Having put in all the effort yesterday to climb out of Glen Tilt, you are well placed for an easy ascent of the first Munro of the day. Pick up the path that you used to ascend out of the glen, then follow it westwards, climbing gradually onto the south-east shoulder of **Carn a'Chlamain.** The path passes close by the summit of Carn a'Chlamain, missing it as it passes over the ridge to the north, and it is an easy matter to bag the top from the path's highest point. The summit of this Munro is at 963m (GR: NN916758). ◀

*Westwards are a couple of very remote hills to climb. The first, **Beinn Mheadhonach**, is a Corbett, while the other, **Beinn Dearg** is a superbly remote Munro.*

To get to Beinn Mheadhonach from Carn a'Chlamain go north-westwards from the summit until you can follow the high ground over the plateau westwards to Aonach na Cloiche Moire. Descend westwards into the head of Gleann Mhairc, then climb out onto the north ridge of Beinn Mheadhonach. Turn south to the summit (GR: NN880758), then return along the ridge and continue northwards to **Carn a'Chiaraidh**. Again keeping to the high ground, you should make for the col to the north-west, and from there climb up and over Elrig 'ic an Toisich (GR: NN867787). Walk westwards over stony ground to the scree-covered north ridge of Beinn Dearg, then turn south to the summit OS trig pillar at 1008m (GR: NN853777).

Southwards from the summit the ridge continues to a big bowl at the head of a stream. A path runs down the eastern arm of this, then turns south into a gully (the Allt Sheicheanan). Follow the path down this gully, following the stream down to a **bothy** near the bottom (GR: NN835736). You could spend a night here if you've had enough.

From the bothy there's a good track running roughly southwards, around the east side of **Meall Dubh**, then crossing the Allt an t-Seapail. Follow this track, continue to the Allt na Moine Baine and then downhill to run alongside the **Banvie Burn**. The track here keeps to the north side of the Banvie Burn, and takes you to the north side of Blair Castle and eventually to the **Old Bridge of Tilt**. Here turn right and follow the lane back into Blair Atholl.

ROUTE 14

The Grampian Glens Grand Traverse

Total Distance	86km
Daily Distances	Day 1 – 21km, Day 2 – 23km, Day 3 – 31km, Day 4 – 11km
Maps	OS Landranger sheet 43 (Braemar & Blair Atholl)
Starting Point	Blair Atholl railway station (GR: NN870653)

Area Summary

A superb backpacking area to the north and east of the A9 at Blair Atholl taking in the great glen country north-eastwards towards Braemar, then the whole southern section of the Cairngorms through to Glen Feshie. The Minigaig pass is an ancient route across the hills back to Blair Atholl.

Route Summary

This route is in complete contrast to the previous one, in that it takes the backpacker through the mighty glens of this part of the Grampians. The route heads north-east up Glen Tilt to the Falls of Tarf, then continues over the watershed to the Geldie Burn. A major through-route westwards is then followed to join up with Glen Feshie before a col is crossed westwards again to link up with Glen Tromie. From there an old drover's route, the Minigaig, is followed southwards, dropping into Glen Bruar, before good tracks are taken back to Blair Atholl.

The route is a superb round of the glens south of the Cairngorms National Park, and is suitable for anyone with a few days to spare who wants to see the best of the region without climbing any mountains. This route could be made into a longer trip by linking up with the Lairig an Laoigh (see Route 5) through to Glen More on the north side of the Cairngorms, then returning to this route either via the Lairig Ghru (see Route 4), or by going westwards to

Glen Feshie, then south along that to gain this route at the bridge near Glenfeshie Lodge. That would make an exceptional multi-day circuit of the Cairngorms.

Tourist Information
The TIC in Pitlochry is great for advice on transport and accommodation. You'll find it on Atholl Road (tel 01796 472215).

Accommodation and Supplies
In Blair Atholl there is the Atholl Arms Hotel (tel 01796 481205), or for a cheaper option stay at the campsite at Blair Castle (tel 01796 481263). There are plenty of other options in Pitlochry – call the TIC for information.

Overnight Options
Camp wild throughout, as the fancy takes you. There are bothies on or near the route that could be used too. The Tarf Hotel (actually a bothy) is off route (GR: NN927788), while Ruigh-aiteachain bothy in Glen Feshie (GR: NN847928) is on the route. Also Allt Sheicheanan bothy (GR: NN835736) in Glen Bruar makes a good place to stay on the final night.

Escape Routes
The glens themselves are the escape routes, but it is worth familiarising yourself with what lies at either end of each glen so that you are aware of the nearest place to make for in an emergency. Basically Glen Tilt leads down to Blair Atholl, and the Geldie Burn leads out to Braemar via Inverey. The Feshie leads northwards to the Spey Valley (Aviemore and Kincraig), while Glen Tromie takes you northwards again (to Kingussie). Once on or over the Minigaig, Glen Bruar leads south to Pitagowan, with tracks linking back to Blair Atholl.

DAY 1
From **Blair Atholl** follow the lane to the **Old Bridge of Tilt**. The lane branches off from the B8079 just to the east of the 'New' Bridge of Tilt. Follow the lane along the east side of the river to the Old Bridge. Go over the bridge and turn right immediately, following the river through woodland until you reach a **bridge**. Walk over the bridge and continue upstream.

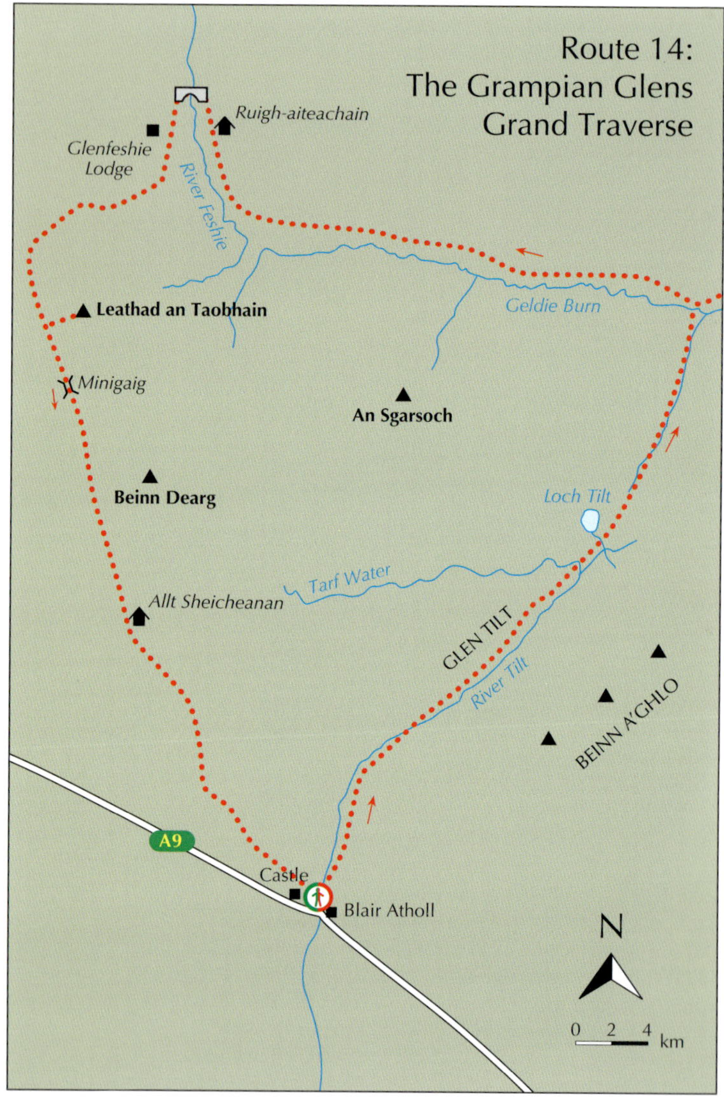
Route 14:
The Grampian Glens
Grand Traverse
Ruigh-aiteachain
Glenfeshie
Lodge
River Feshie
Leathad an Taobhain
Geldie Burn
Minigaig
An Sgarsoch
Loch Tilt
Beinn Dearg
Tarf Water
Allt Sheicheanan
GLEN TILT
River Tilt
BEINN A'GHLO
A9
Castle
Blair Atholl
N
0   2   4 km

At the next bridge, **Gilbert's Bridge**, stay on the east side of the River Tilt, and continue to Auchgobhal, then walk on to Marble Lodge. Do not cross the river at the bridge just beyond the Lodge, but instead stay on the path up the east side as far as Balaneasie. Cross the bridge here, and turn right up the glen, continuing to Clachghlas.

The route up the spectacular glen is very obvious, taking you first to Forest Lodge, in its belt of trees, then onwards below the screes of Creag a'Chrochaidh. As you walk past Creag a'Chrochaidh look up the glen on the left side. There is a small, rocky knoll overhanging the river on the left, 3km up the glen, known as Dun Beag. As you approach this knoll, the track swings up the gully to the west of Dun Beag, but you want to stay below the Dun, close by the river. There is a path along here, leaving the main track 1km short of Dun Beag.

Keeping close by the River Tilt throughout, the path swings sharply to the north 1km beyond Dun Beag, and here enters a spectacular gorge. In a short while the side stream of the River Tarf gushes into the Tilt, and there is a bridge over the Tarf.

This is a wonderful place to camp for the night, if you can find a flat spot, although some might find the closeness of the gorge, and the constant noise from the river at the Falls of Tarf a little off-putting.

DAY 2

Continue just north of east through the gorge of the upper Tilt. This upper stream is known as the Allt Garbh Buidhe, and as you near the watershed you'll spot a knoll to its left with a cairn on the highest point (GR: NN997828). The path passes to the right of this knoll, but a more interesting diversion goes to the left of the knoll, visiting **Loch Tilt**, the source of the River Tilt. The loch sits in a wonderful moorland setting, and if you didn't camp at the Falls of Tarf last night, would make a great spot for a camp site.

An Sgarsoch to the south of the Geldie Burn

Walk north-eastwards, around the north side of the knoll, and regain the path. Continue northwards down to the ruins at **Bynack Lodge**, then walk on to the banks of the **Geldie Burn**. Here you must cross to the north side of the river, which invariably involves fording (there isn't a bridge at this point).

If the Geldie Burn is in spate you should consider whether it is better to camp on the south side until the water level is lower and you can cross safely, or walk downstream (north-east) for 2km to White Bridge where there is another footbridge over the Geldie.

The way here is very open and wild, and you get great views into the northern flanks and corries of the Atholl Munros.

Once on the north side of the Geldie Burn turn westwards along the track. ◀

Where the track swings down towards the river to cross to Geldie Lodge, you'll notice a path continuing westwards, and should take this, keeping on the north side of the Geldie Burn.

Crossing a bridge at the head of Glen Feshie

As you pass below the broad southern flanks of Cnapan Mor, you pass above the headwaters of the Geldie Burn. The **River Feshie** swings in from the south and curves around the west here, and you will have to cross a side stream via a bridge before you can drop down to the banks of the river.

The Feshie is stunningly beautiful and immediately the glen begins to close in. There are a few delectable camp sites by the river, beneath the shade of ancient Scot's pine trees, and you can choose from any number of great places to pitch up for the night, or continue to the bothy at Ruigh-aiteachain.

DAY 3

If you camped last night you'll want to continue along the east side of the River Feshie to the **bothy** at **Ruigh-aiteachain**. There are two tracks here, and to continue you need to take the one nearest to the river as this leads to a bridge over the Feshie (GR: NN846937). Cross the rickety bridge and turn left onto the drive to **Glenfeshie Lodge**. Walk southwards, past the Lodge for 1.5km to a

ruin where the track turns to the south-west (there is a junction here, with a path going off to the south, but you don't need to take that).

Follow the track south-westwards up into the lovely little runnel holding **Lochan an t-Sluic**, and 500m beyond the lochan you'll reach a junction. Turn right down to a stream. Just beyond the stream there is a path shooting off on the left into a plantation (the main track climbs steeply here dead ahead), and you should take this path going westwards. It climbs gently at first, and then contours through the plantation and out the other side. Continue along the path and into another plantation, and then turn left where the path regains the main track as it swings back down hill on the edge of the wood. Follow the edge of the wood westwards, then south, keeping on the path throughout.

Walk southwards on a good path as it climbs alongside a burn towards a shoulder of **Leathad an Taobhain**.

The path gets steeper as it passes to the west of this fine little Corbett. You can easily deviate from the path to climb to the summit at 912m (GR: NN822858). ▸

The path here is very obvious and drops down to cross a burn before contouring over the eastern side of Uchd a'Chlarsair. It then drops steeply down to the south into the head of Glen Bruar.

There is now a good track on the east side of the Bruar Water, and you should follow this through to **Bruar Lodge**. At the lodge you'll see a bridge where the main track swings over to the west bank. Ignore this and pick up a path that continues southwards along the east side of the river. Initially this keep to the flat valley bottom, but then it climbs gently around the flanks of **Druim Dubh** before you descend slightly to the **Allt Sheicheanan bothy** (GR: NN835736).

DAY 4

From the Allt Sheicheanan bothy there's a good track running roughly southwards. Follow this around the east side of **Meall Dubh**, then cross the Allt an t-Seapail. Continue along the track to cross the Allt na Moine Baine and then walk downhill to the banks of the **Banvie Burn**. The track here keeps to the north side of the Banvie Burn, and takes you to the north side of **Blair Castle** and eventually to the **Old Bridge of Tilt**. Here turn right and follow the lane back into Blair Atholl.

The **Minigaig** Pass, where the path climbs over the south-west flank of Leathad an Taobhain (GR: NN812847), is an important crossing point that has been used for centuries.

ROUTE 15

The Scottish 4000'ers Traverse

Total Distance	143km
Daily Distances	Day 1 – 18km, Day 2 – 22km, Day 3 – 28km, Day 4 – 14km, Day 5 – 19km, Day 6 – 24km, Day 7 – 18km
Maps	OS Landranger sheets 36 (Grantown & Aviemore), 43 (Braemar & Blair Atholl), 42 (Glen Garry & Loch Rannoch), and 41 (Ben Nevis). Also Harvey British Mountain Maps 1:40,000 scale (Cairngorms & Lochnagar, and Ben Nevis & Glen Coe).
Starting Point	Glenmore Forest Park (GR: NH977097), east of Aviemore. There is a free car park just south-east of the Forest Park Visitor Centre, at GR NH980093). Do not park in the Visitor Centre car park, as this is pay and display.
Finishing Point	Fort William (GR: NN105742)

Area Summary

A grand traverse of all the mountains of Scotland that reach the giddy heights of 4000 feet. There are nine Munros on the current list of tables that qualify, and this route crosses the country from east to west to climb all of them in one backpacking trip. The Cairngorms, Gaick Forest, Ben Alder Forest, Rannoch Moor, the Grey Corries, the Aonachs, and finally Ben Nevis are all crossed before Fort William is reached. Most days take the high route where one is available, whereas on others the walking in mainly on low-level paths.

Route Summary

From Glenmore Forest Park the Cairngorms are tackled. Cairngorm itself is climbed first, and then Ben Macdui before the Lairig Ghru is crossed to gain the Braeriach group. The second day sees Braeriach, Sgor an Lochain

The path up the Faicaill a'Choire Chais to Cairngorm

Tourist Information

Grampian Road, Aviemore (tel 01479 810363); Cameron Square, Fort William (tel 01397 703781).

Accommodation and Supplies

Lots of options in Aviemore and Fort William, with good youth hostels in both places too (tel 08701 553255 Central Reservations, www.syha.org.uk). The only place to restock with food supplies along the route is Dalwhinnie, and there your options are very limited. It is best to carry enough food and fuel for the entire duration of your trip.

Overnight Options

Camp throughout along the route. Other options include the bothies at Garbh Coire (GR: NN959986), Ruigh-aiteachain in Glen Feshie (GR: NN847928), Culra in the Ben Alder Forest (GR: NN523762), and at Lairig Leacach at the eastern end of the Grey Corries (GR: NN283736). The SYHA hostel at Loch Ossian (GR: NN371670) is a great place to spend the night (contact as above), as is the Inn at Dalwhinnie (tel 01528 522257, www.theinndalwhinnie.com).

Escape Routes

These are too numerous to list for such a long route. As a rough guide, the Lairig Ghru, Glen Feshie and Glen Tromie are all good options, then it's over to the A9 and Dalwhinnie. The railway line at Corrour (just west of Loch Ossian) is useful too, then once you've headed north-west towards the Grey Corries the best option is to head down Glen Nevis, running west to the south of the main Grey Corries ridge.

Uaine, and Cairn Toul being climbed before an adventurous crossing of Am Moine Mhor is undertaken to reach Glen Feshie. The third day is a long one, taking you westwards over the Gaick Forest to the A9 at Dalwhinnie, before the long shores of Loch Ericht are followed to Culra in the Ben Alder Forest. Through the Ben Alder Forest to Loch Ossian, then over Rannoch Moor to the eastern end of the Grey Corries ridge, the route then takes you on a magnificent traverse of these hills (all of them Munros, but not quite 4000 feet) to a high camp below Aonach Beag. The final day sees you crossing Aonach Beag and Aonach Mor before tackling the Carn Mor Dearg Arête up to the summit of Ben Nevis, then it's just a stroll down into Fort William. Superb.

DAY 1

Begin by walking along the footpath that follows the road southwards towards the Cairngorm Mountain Ski Centre. There is a path all the way, first running along the east side of the road, then switching from side to side as you climb. Your objective is the Coire Cas car park (GR: NH990060), up in the northern corries of **Cairngorm**. Pass to the right of the Ranger Base, then left of the café area. There is a stone track here that soon runs alongside the funicular. Before leaving the cluster of buildings behind you'll see a phone box by the side of this track. On the right at this point is a small path that climbs up eastwards onto the heathery ridge of Sron an Aonaich. Follow this path, turning right up the ridge, and you'll find yourself climbing quickly towards the Ptarmigan restaurant (GR: NJ004049).

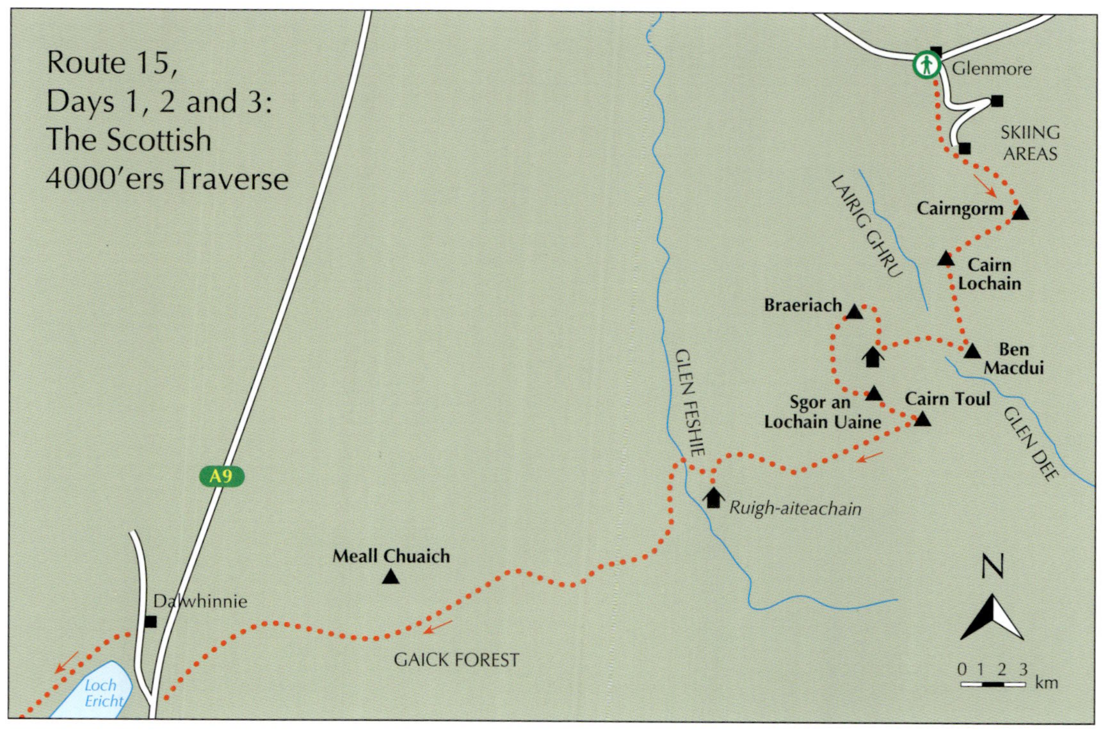
Route 15,
Days 1, 2 and 3:
The Scottish
4000'ers Traverse
Glenmore
SKIING AREAS
LAIRIG GHRU
Cairngorm
Cairn Lochain
Braeriach
Ben Macdui
Cairn Toul
GLEN DEE
Sgor an Lochain Uaine
GLEN FESHIE
Ruigh-aiteachain
A9
Meall Chuaich
Dalwhinnie
GAICK FOREST
Loch Ericht
N
0 1 2 3 km

Cairngorm

Walk around to the south side of the Ptarmigan Restaurant. There's a major track cutting across the slopes here. Ignore this track and follow a paved path and line of cairn due south, climbing steadily to the summit of Cairngorm at 1245m (GR: NJ005041).

Cairngorm's summit has a small automated weather station, while the summit cairn lies just to the north. Head south-west from the summit and you'll pick up a path leading down to a large cairn at 1141m. South of here the ridge is quite bouldery and has the cliffs of **Coire an t-Sneachda** to the north-west. Keep the top of these cliffs to your right and handrail around to the summit of Stob Coire an t-Sneachda at 1176m. Drop down just south of west to a stony col at the very head of Coire an t-Sneachda ◀

*Southwards the plateau opens up towards **Ben Macdui**, Britain's second highest mountain.*

Now climb westwards, following the cliffs of Coire an Lochain to the summit of **Cairn Lochan** at 1215m.

Descend to the broad col at the head of the March Burn. From here a bouldery path leads south-eastwards to the top of Ben Macdui at 1309m (GR: NN989989).

Head north-west from the summit of Ben Macdui, picking up a ridge above the burn of the Allt a'Choire Mhoir.

There's a memorial on the top of this ridge to the air-crew of a British Services plane that crashed here during the 1940s.

Descend steep slopes to the west alongside the Allt a'Choire Mhoir, down into the **Lairig Ghru**. The way is rough, with lots of scree, but if you take it carefully this is an easy way down.

You should hit the Lairig Ghru path at a point where it leaves the side of the infant River Dee and cuts diagonally across the slopes to the south-east.

From this point cross the river, then contour around to the west on roughly the 680m contour. This will lead you into the **Garbh Coire** of Braeriach where you can camp for the night, ready for a long day tomorrow.

DAY 2

The walk today begins with a long and steep climb up onto the Braeriach plateau. Head for the east side of **Coire Bhrochain** to gain the plateau on the ridge between Sron na Lairig and the summit of **Braeriach** (GR: NN962999). Another option is to go north-west up the spur to the west of Coire Bhrochain, and so to the summit from there.

The summit trig pillar on Ben Macdui

Braeriach's top lies at 1296m right on the edge of the cliffs overlooking Coire Bhrochain (GR: NN953999). From the top, skirt around the head of a big gully cutting into the plateau to the south-west, then head south-west across the plateau to the rim of cliffs overlooking Garbh Coire. Follow this line of cliffs, handrailing around the corrie rim to the south and west, until you reach the broad flat top of Carn na Criche at 1265m. ◄

To get to the Angel's Peak summit you need to continue around the rim of the plateau keeping the cliffs of Garbh Choire Mor close by as a guide all the way.

Sgor an Lochain Uaine is a fabulous peak, and its summit at 1258m is a great place to relax for a while and enjoy the views back across the corrie to Braeraich.

Slightly higher than Sgor an Lochain Uaine is **Cairn Toul** (GR: NN963972), lying a short way off to the south-east. Drop down into the col between the two, then climb easily up to the summit at 1291m.

Now, aiming for the wild wastes of Am Moine Mor and the route westwards to Lochaber, head south-westwards from Cairn Toul, being careful not to be drawn too far downhill as you walk across the headwaters of the Allt Clais an t-Sabhail. The route continues westwards, passing close by the north shores of Loch nan Stuirteag (GR: NN941958), and the south side of **Loch nan Cnapan** (GR: NN917960) with the little lump of Tom Dumb rising to the south.

Just a short way west of Loch nan Cnapan there is a burn gurgling over the moor, and here you'll pick up a path heading west. This soon curves to the south-west and you should follow it in a bend around the rim of **Coire Garbhlach** to a junction (GR: NN883936). Turn right here and descend easily into the beautiful **Glen Feshie**.

As you descend towards the river in the glen you could start to think about camping for the night. Another option is to use the **bothy** at **Ruigh-aiteachain** (GR: NN847928) which lies along a path to the south.

DAY 3

From Ruigh-aiteachain head north to the bridge over the River Feshie. Cross over and walk southwards, passing **Glenfeshie Lodge** and continuing for 1.5km to a ruin where the track turns to the south-west (there is a junction here, with a path going off to the south, but you don't need to take that).

Follow the track south-westwards up into the lovely little runnel holding **Lochan an t-Sluic**, and 500m beyond the lochan you'll reach a junction. Turn right down to a stream. Just beyond the stream there is a path shooting off on the left into a plantation (the main track climbs steeply here dead ahead), and you should take this path going westwards. It climbs gently at first, and then contours through the plantation and out the other side. Continue along the path and into another plantation, and then turn left where the path regains the main track as it swings back down hill on the edge of the wood. Follow the edge of the wood westwards, then south, keeping on the path throughout until you come to the western-most point of the plantation (GR: NN800890). A little further south, across the Allt na Cuilce is a path junction, but as you want to be on the

Ruigh-aiteachain bothy in Glen Feshie

121

north side of the Allt Bhran heading west you can just cut the corner off, rather than cross the Allt na Cuilce.

Follow the path on the north side of the Allt Bhran until it comes to a little **weir** where you can cross over. A path then crosses the moor to the south-west to gain the main track through the **Gaick Forest** (GR: NN765888). Turn right along the track for 100m, then head down to the River Tromie where there is a bridge leading over to the west side.

You now have some very rough moorland walking ahead. Take a bearing for the col to the south of **Meall Chuaich** (GR: NN721868), and bash through the heather towards it, over the northern flanks of Bogha-cloiche.

At the col, and if you're feeling fit, you could nip up Meall Chuaich (at 951m, it's a Munro) to the north, then return to the col to resume the route.

On the west side of the col is a track which you should follow along the north side of the Allt Coire Chuaich, crossing over just before **Loch Chuaich**. Then follow the very obvious track out to Dalwhinnie, going westwards along the river.

DAY 4

An easier day than the others so far on this trip. Start by walking to the northern end of **Dalwhinnie**, then turning left towards the **train station**. Bear left and cross the tracks then follow the track that runs along the north side of **Loch Ericht**. This is now a much-improved track, and there are a number of new houses and lodges along the side of the loch.

Continue along the track to a junction (GR: NN575792), just short of **Ben Alder** Lodge. Turn right here and continuing to a bridge over a burn where you emerge from the forests. Here another path to the right leaves the main track, but you should ignore this and walk on, just south of westwards. Within 1.4km take a path on the left. Walk westwards along it then follow it as it bends around to the south-west and drops to the

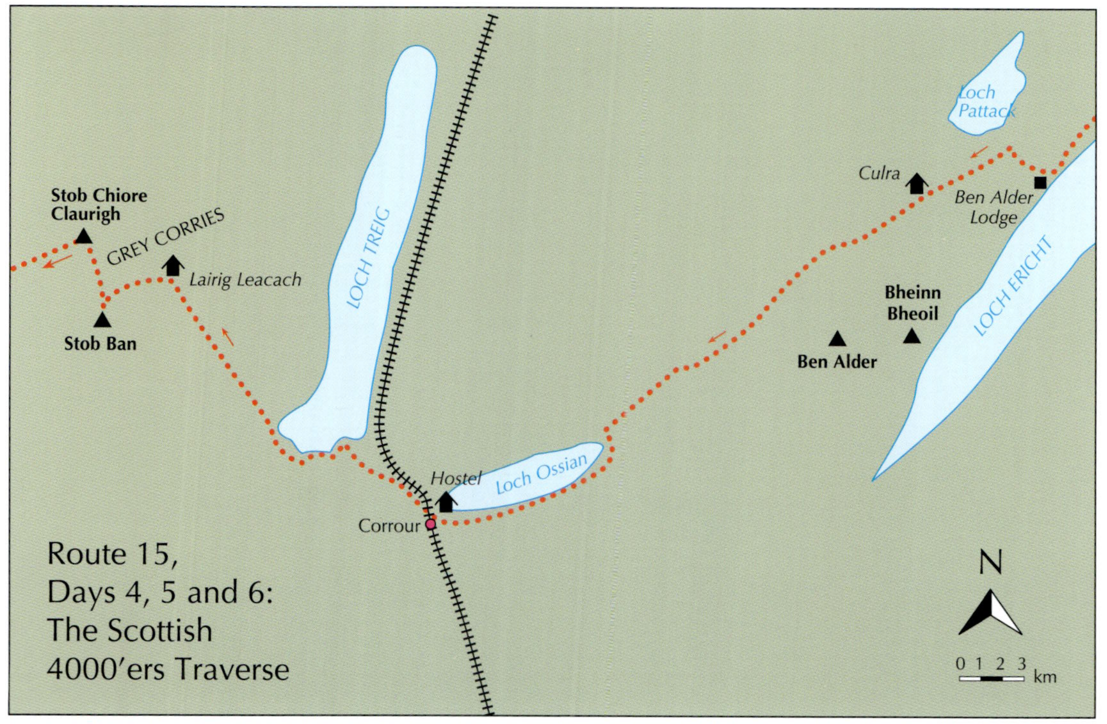
Stob Chiore Claurigh
GREY CORRIES
Lairig Leacach
Stob Ban
LOCH TREIG
Loch Pattack
Culra
Ben Alder Lodge
LOCH ERICHT
Bheinn Bheoil
Ben Alder
Hostel
Loch Ossian
Corrour
N
0 1 2 3 km
Route 15, Days 4, 5 and 6: The Scottish 4000'ers Traverse

banks of the Allt a'Chaoil-reidhe. Follow the river upstream until you reach a bridge just short of the bothy at **Culra** (GR: NN523762).

DAY 5

Staying on the north side of the river, leave Culra bothy and follow the track south-westwards to the top of the deep col at **Bealach Dubh** (GR: NN481732). Walk through the pass that sits tightly beneath **Ben Alder** to the south and **Aonach Beag** to the north.

Once over the pass the path starts to cut across the slopes to the south-west, rather than just descending into the valley, and after a while you'll want to leave this higher path to drop down and pick up the lower one in the bottom of the glen. The lower path follows the Uisge Labhair on its north side until you come to a bridge (GR: NN417702). Cross the bridge, then follow a path to the south-west, entering a forest plantation. Bear left here on a track that leads down to another track by the lochside.

At the main track that goes around **Loch Ossian** turn left, following the track around the loch in a clockwise direction. Stay close by the edge of the loch. At the south-western corner there is a junction and a path swings off to the right to take you to the **SYHA hostel**. This is a great place to spend the night.

DAY 6

A long day lies ahead, and you may well want to split it into two, perhaps staying overnight at the Lairig Leacach Bothy.

From the hostel walk back out to the main track and turn right. At the next junction, within 500m, turn right again (the track straight ahead goes to the train station at **Corrour**). Within another 300m, just around a sharp bend to the right, there is a path on the left which you should take. Follow the path north-westwards, going under the railway line at a bridge (GR: NN342681). On the west side of the railway line the path becomes more of a track and you should follow this to the southern shore of **Loch Treig** where a bridge takes you over a river

(GR: NN327690). Continue westwards along the track to the outflow of the Abhainn Rath where a bridge takes you over to **Creaguaineach Lodge**. Again the path splits. To the left the route takes you towards Glen Nevis, while your route goes straight on. There's another bridge on the right 300m away. Ignore this and stay on the west side of the Alt na Lairige until you reach the **Lairig Leacach Bothy** (GR: NN283736).

Climb steeply up into the corrie to the west, above the bothy. This leads to a col below the pointed cone of **Stob Ban**, and from the col you could head up southwards to climb this great little Munro.

Back at the col the rest of the Grey Corries ridge is waiting to be traversed. Climb northwards up the steep slopes of **Stob Choire Claurigh** to the summit at 1177m (GR: NN263738). ▶

Follow the ridge over **Stob a'Choire Leith** at 1105m, Stob Coire Cath na Sine at 1079m, **Caisteil** at 1106m, and carry on to **Stob Coire an Laoigh**, at 1116m (GR: NN240725). Now the ridge veers away to the north-west to the sharp top of **Stob Coire Easain** at 1080m, before turning back to the south-west to take you up the final Munro of the Grey Corries, **Sgurr Choinnich Mor**, at 1094m (GR: NN227714).

There are no less than 11 distinct 3000-feet summits along the Grey Corries ridge, but surprisingly only four of them count as Munros – Stob Ban, Stob Choire Claurigh, Stob Coire an Laoigh, and Sgurr Choinnich Mor.

South-west from Sgurr Choinnich Mor there is the final peak of the range to cross before you can camp for the night – this is **Sgurr Choinnich Beag** at 963m. Drop down off the west ridge of Sgurr Choinnich Beag to a col at 731m, high above Coire Bhealaidh, and find somewhere around here to camp for the night (GR: NN213706).

Westwards the ridge curves away, climbing and dipping over a number of superb peaks.

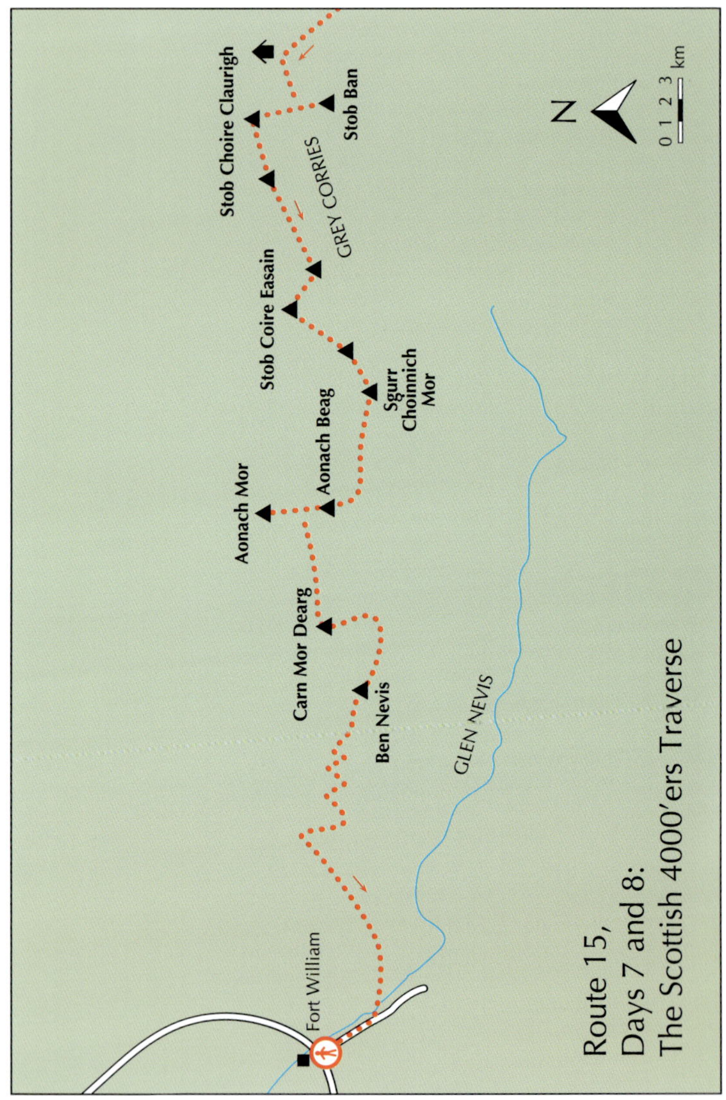
Stob Choire Claurigh
Stob Ban
GREY CORRIES
Stob Coire Easain
Aonach Beag
Sgurr Choinnich Mor
Aonach Mor
Carn Mor Dearg
Ben Nevis
GLEN NEVIS
Fort William
N
0 1 2 3 km
Route 15,
Days 7 and 8:
The Scottish 4000'ers Traverse

DAY 7

This final day is the most spectacular of the route, and will take you over the remaining 4000-foot peaks of Scotland, terminating on the summit of Ben Nevis itself.

Start from the col where you ended yesterday by climbing westwards up the impressive Stob Coire Bhealaich face of Aonach Beag. Initially this looks as if it is going to be very difficult, but in practise the going is quite easy. You soon find yourself on a fine jagged ridge, walking to the summit of **Stob Coire Bhealaich** at 1101m. The big cliffs to your right act as a guide and you can handrail along the rim of these to the summit of **Aonach Beag** at 1234m (GR: NN197715).

A path now leads north-westwards down to a col and from there easy ground rises to the north, levelling out greatly as you approach the summit of **Aonach Mor** at 1221m (GR: NN193729).

The Tower Ridge of Ben Nevis, looking westwards from the summit

127

There are some steep rocky bulges on the ridge up to the summit, but you can stay to the right of these to ease the way up.

Return southwards towards the col between Aonach Mor and Aonach Beag, but do not descend all the way down into this. Instead, 800m south of the summit of Aonach Mor, you should take a bearing to the west. This leads down via some rough ground to another col at 830m (GR: NN187723), and from there it is a direct ascent to the summit of **Carn Mor Dearg** at 1220m. ◄ The summit is marked by a large cairn on the edge of the knife-edge ridge (GR: NN177722).

The route to the summit of **Ben Nevis**, the highest mountain in all of the British Isles, now lies easily ahead. Turn southwards from the summit of Carn Mor Dearg, descending an ever narrowing ridge. Some grade 1 scrambling is needed along here, but is never too difficult, even with a big pack on your back.

The ridge curves gradually around to the south-west, and drops to a stony col at the head of **Coire Leis**. Follow the rim of the crags on the right for a while, then climb up steep, bouldery slopes to the north-west, gaining the Ben Nevis summit plateau above the North East Buttress and Little Brenva Face. The summit is very obvious with a large cairn, and a shelter at 1334m (GR: NN167713).

After celebrating having climbed all the 4000′ mountains of Britain, you need to be thinking about the route down. The summit plateau of Ben Nevis is a notoriously difficult place to navigate around in bad visibility, as enormous gullies cut into the flat top, and many of these have huge cornices hiding the big drops beneath. Bad weather and wintry storms can affect Ben Nevis at any time of year, and cornices can last well into the summer. The Harvey British Mountain Map to Ben Nevis is particularly useful here as it has a 1:15,000 scale map of the Ben Nevis summit area on the rear of the standard map.

To descend to the Red Burn path and Fort William, follow a Grid Bearing of 231° for 150m, and then a Grid Bearing of 282° until you hit the zigzags of the Red Burn path.

The Red Burn path, also known as the Mountain Track, the Easy Route, or the Tourist Route, takes you down in long, gradual zigzags to a crossing of the Red Burn (GR: NN147718), then onwards to a junction at a big cairn overlooking **Lochan Meall an t-Suidhe** (GR: NN147724). Turn left here and follow the obvious path down into **Glen Nevis**.

Low down in the glen the path splits (GR: NN133720). Turn left for the Glen Nevis Youth Hostel, and a stroll along the road into **Fort William**, or go straight ahead for Achintee Farm, and a shorter route into Fort William.

Descending the Red Burn track off Ben Nevis

ROUTE 16

The Ben Alder Forest

Total Distance	50km
Daily Distances	Day 1 – 25km, Day 2 – 25km
Maps	OS Landranger sheets 42 (Glen Garry & Loch Rannoch), and 41 (Ben Nevis)
Starting Point	Corrour Station, on the line between Glasgow and Fort William (GR: NN355664)

Area Summary

A beautiful and wild region, benefiting from the easy access provided by the West Highland Railway Line. There are countless opportunities within these wild hills to extend the number of days spent exploring, and either of the routes taken on these two days could also be combined with the 4000'ers Traverse (see Route 15) to provide an alternative to walking through the Ben Alder Forest by crossing the Bealach Dubh. The region is sandwiched between the A9 at Dalwhinnie, and the West Highland railway line. To the north Loch Treig and the Ardverikie Forest form natural boundaries, while to the south-east Loch Ericht does likewise.

Route Summary

The route takes in the remote Munros to the north of Loch Ossian, a lovely loch that sits at the heart of this region. The route traverses these Munros from west to east, finally descending at Culra Bothy. On Day 2 you climb Ben Alder itself before returning to Corrour Station via the shores of Loch Ossian.

DAY 1

From **Corrour** station walk eastwards on a good track that leads towards **Loch Ossian**. As you approach the western end of the loch there is another track branching

Tourist Information
Cameron Square, Fort William (tel 01397 703781).

Accommodation and Supplies
Lots of options in Fort William, with a good hostel in Glen Nevis too (tel 08701 553255 Central Reservations, website www.syha.org.uk).

Overnight Options
Camp along the route, or use Culra bothy in the Ben Alder Forest (GR: NN523762). The SYHA hostel at Loch Ossian (GR: NN371670) is a great place to spend the night (contact as above).

Escape Routes
Head west via Loch Ossian to Corrour Station, or east to Dalwhinnie and the A9.

off to the left and you should follow this, clockwise around Loch Ossian until you are on the northern shore. Before you reach the extensive forestry plantations that cloak the shore break out northwards off the track, climbing steeply to gain the long west ridge of **Beinn na**

Climbing Beinn na Lap

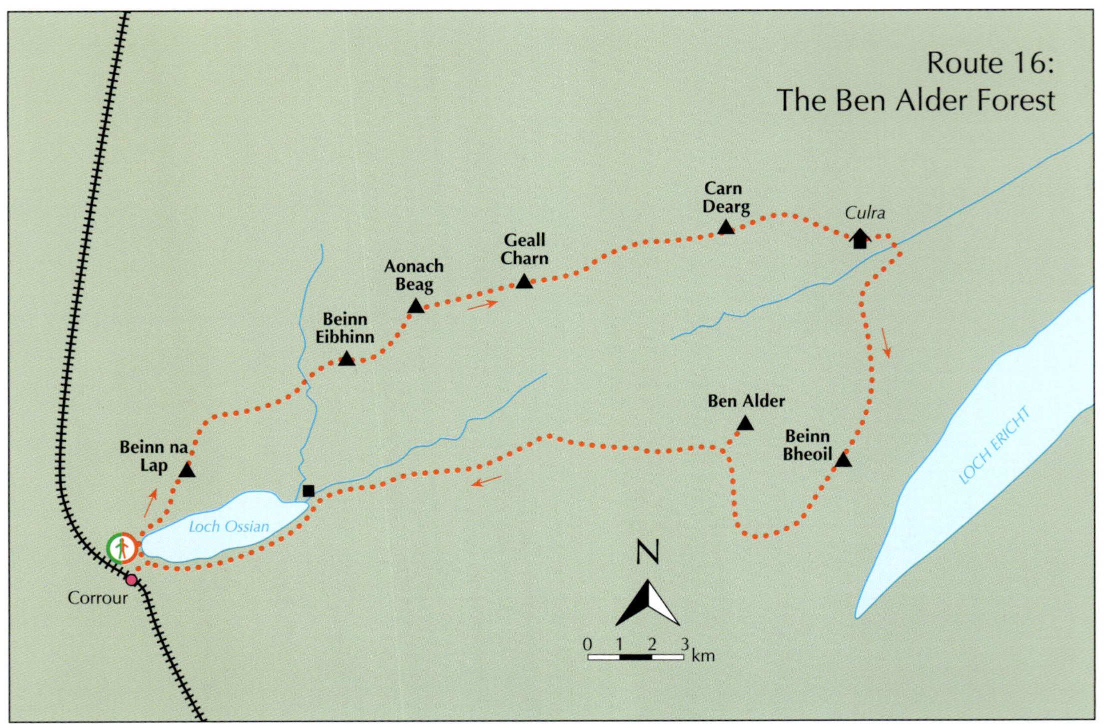

Route 16:
The Ben Alder Forest
Carn Dearg
Culra
Geall Charn
Aonach Beag
Beinn Eibhinn
Ben Alder
Beinn Bheoil
LOCH ERICHT
Beinn na Lap
Loch Ossian
Corrour
N
0 1 2 3 km

Lap. Turn eastwards up this ridge to reach the summit cairn at 935m (GR: NN376695).

There is a superb north ridge off Beinn na Lap, with steep ground falling away to Loch na Lap to the east. From the summit, head just east of north down the obvious ridge. This is never too narrow, and gives a pleasant descent to **Strath Ossian**. Once at the bottom of the ridge turn right along a path to reach a track at a bridge over the Allt Feith Thuill. Turn right along this track, and follow it to another path junction. If you look down to the river from this point you'll see a bridge over the River Ossian (GR: NN410727). There is a path leading down to this bridge, and once over on the east side of the river you should start climbing up the steep slopes to the east. Your objective is the rough, rocky ridge of Creagan nan Nead, and you should gain this at a flat area on top of the steeper section (GR: NN422728). From this small flat area turn to the north-east and climb up to the spot height at 921m (GR: NN430734). Immediately east of this little top there are two tarns on the ridge, one draining northwards, and the other southwards. Head over to the narrow gap between these two lochan, then continue climbing eastwards up the broad ridge of **Beinn Eibhinn**. The summit ridge curves above a rocky north-east facing corrie, and once you reach the upper rim of this you can turn to the south-east and handrail along until you get to the summit cairn at 1100m (GR: NN449733).

The next summit is, like Beinn Eibhinn, a Munro, and a high ridge connects the two. Head eastwards from Beinn Eibhinn, curving round and down a narrow ridge to a col, then climb the south-west arête of **Aonach Beag** to its top at 1114m (GR: NN458742).

Eastwards again another Munro awaits, and it's a simple matter of dropping down to a col immediately east of Aonach Beag's summit, then continue just north of east to the plateau-like top of **Geall Charn** at 1132m (GR: NN470746). Interestingly, this is the highest Munro on this north side of the glen, and yet the Ordnance Survey does not name it on the Landranger map.

Head just north of east again, walking across the open plateau of Geall-Charn for 1km, until you reach the top of a narrow, steep spur jutting down to a col (GR: NN480751). To the north of this spur is **Loch Coire Cheap**, while to the south the lower **Loch an Sgoir** fills the corrie.

Scramble carefully down the rocky spur to a narrow but level section of ridge, then climb up to the minor top of Diollaid a'Chairn at 922m (GR: NN487758). Now the long west ridge of **Carn Dearg** presents itself. Follow this over stony ground to the summit of the final Munro of the day at 1034m (GR: NN504764).

Culra bothy lies due east of the summit of Carn Dearg, but to get there it is best to first head north-east along the ridge for 1km, then descend easier slopes to the south-east to reach the bothy.

DAY 2

Just downstream of Culra bothy there is a **bridge** giving access to the south side of the Allt a'Chaoil-reidhe. Cross the bridge, then head back up the other side of the river, going south-westwards. As the path begins to climb to the south, away from the river, you can leave it and head south-eastwards to gain the long northern spur of **Beinn Bheoil** at a flat section on the ridge (GR: NN522736).

Once on the ridge turn southwards and follow it, initially over an intervening bump, then up a narrow arête to the summit of this fine Munro, Beinn Bheoil, at 1019m (GR: NN517717).

Go south-westwards from the summit for 500m, then continue down a narrow ridge to a col. Climb up the other side to a subsidiary top, Sron Coire na h-Iolaire at 955m, then turn west and descend sharply to the **Bealach Breabag** (GR: NN507703), the wide col that lies at the high point between Beinn Bheoil and Ben Alder.

The route up **Ben Alder** from here is straightforward, though steep at first. Climb west for 500m, then north-west to a rise on the south ridge. Huge cliffs drop away to the north-east from the rim of the plateau, and you can handrail around these to the north-west to reach a little

Geall Charn's Lancet Edge from Culra Bothy (Route 16)

tarn, **Lochan a'Garbh Choire** (GR: NN495715), tucked into a little fold high on the summit plateau of Ben Alder. The summit of this fine Munro lies just 500m away across the plateau to the north-east. The top has an OS trig pillar at 1148m (GR: NN496718).

From the summit, turn westwards, descending very gradually at first to a ring contour after 1.5km. Below this knoll, and still to the west, the ground falls away more steeply to a rocky ridge. Follow this down into the head of the glen.

There is a path down in the bottom of the glen that follows the Uisge Labhair on its north side until you come to a bridge (GR: NN417702). Cross the bridge then bear right immediately, aiming for the corner of a wood just above Corrour Shooting Lodge. At the main track that goes around Loch Ossian turn left, following the track around the loch in a clockwise direction. Stay close by the edge of the loch. At the south-western corner there is a junction and a path swings off to the right to the SYHA hostel. Ignore this unless you plan on spending the night here, and carry on westwards to another junction. Take the left track back to Corrour Station.

ROUTE 17
The Glen Nevis High Level Traverse

Total Distance	57km
Daily Distances	Day 1 – 32km, Day 2 – 25km
Maps	Harvey British Mountain Map 1:40,000 (Ben Nevis & Glen Coe).
Starting Point	Glen Nevis Youth Hostel (GR: NN127717).

Area Summary

The stunning mountains on either side of Glen Nevis, running eastwards from Fort William. A number of important mountain ranges are traversed on this route, including the Mamores, the Grey Corries, the Aonachs, and Ben Nevis itself. This is a high mountain route that is suitable only for those with experience both of backpacking, and of the highest Munros. Navigational ability is required, as is the experience to pick a suitable and safe escape route from off rugged and rocky mountains.

Route Summary

This is the trip of a lifetime for any Munro-bagger (the route described takes you over no less than 18 Munros), and includes the traverses of two of Scotland's finest ridges, the Mamores, and the Grey Corries. The route described here is for those wanting to tackle this challenging round of Glen Nevis in just two days, although of course many would find that this would make a worthy challenge over four or even five days. Going to the other extreme, fell runners tackle this route, known as Tranter's Round, in under 24 hours!

Tourist Information

Cameron Square, Fort William (tel 01397 703781)

Accommodation and Supplies
Lots of options in Fort William, with a good hostel in Glen Nevis too (tel 08701 553255 Central Reservations, www.syha.org.uk).

Overnight Options
Camp along the route, or use the bothy at Meanach (GR: NN266685) on the north side of the Abhainn Rath.

Escape Routes
The obvious escape route is Glen Nevis itself, although depending on where you are on the traverse it may make sense to head east to Corrour Station, or even south into Kinlochleven.

DAY 1
This is a magnificent expedition, taking in the fell runners classic Tranter's Round.

Tranter's Round was the original 24-hour challenge. Although it has now been superseded by the longer Ramsay's Round, it is still a wonderful expedition for all. The 40-mile route (with 20,600 feet of ascent) takes in the Mamores plus the Grey Corries, Aonachs, and Ben Nevis, and was first achieved by Philip Tranter in June 1964. Mark McDermott set the record of 12 hours 50 minutes, when he did the round solo and unsupported in 1990, while the ladies record is believed to be held by Dawn Scott in a time of 15hrs 57 minutes. She went anticlockwise, finishing off the Ben just after daybreak on 19 July 2000.

Start from the **youth hostel**, turning left out of the door and heading down Glen Nevis. Within 200m you will come to a footpath on the left, heading uphill, and you should take this into the forestry plantation until you reach a track cutting across the hillside. Turn left here. Follow this track up Glen Nevis now, until you emerge from the trees after 4km.

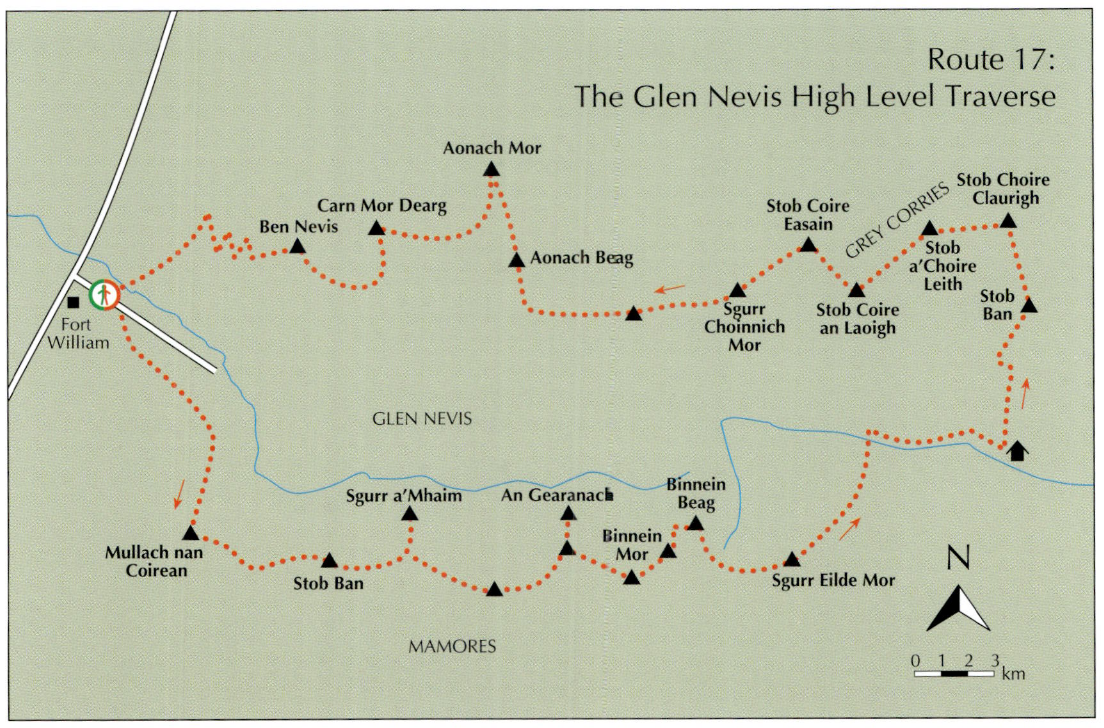

Route 17:
The Glen Nevis High Level Traverse
Aonach Mor
Carn Mor Dearg
Ben Nevis
Aonach Beag
Stob Coire Easain
GREY CORRIES
Stob Choire Claurigh
Stob a'Choire Leith
Stob Ban
Sgurr Choinnich Mor
Stob Coire an Laoigh
Fort William
GLEN NEVIS
Sgurr a'Mhaim
An Gearanach
Binnein Beag
Binnein Mor
Mullach nan Coirean
Stob Ban
Sgurr Eilde Mor
MAMORES
N
0 1 2 3 km

From here you can head up the stream to the right for a short way, then move up onto the steep ridge that comes down to the west from the summit of **Mullach nan Coirean**. This ridge is boggy lower down, but has a good path the higher you get. It curves around the summit crags, depositing you on the small summit plateau. Handrail around to the top at 939m (GR: NN123662).

Walk south-east along the ridge, keeping the crags and steep ground to your left as you go. The path takes you over a minor top at 917m, then eastwards along an undulating ridge to the pointed summit of **Stob Ban** at 999m (GR: NN147654).

The east ridge of Stob Ban is steep and a little rocky in places, but nowhere is it particularly difficult. It leads down to a col where the path cuts across the open bowl of a corrie holding the tiny Lochan Coire nam Miseach. Follow the path past this tarn, then zigzag up the steep slopes opposite to the edge of a narrow ridge. This is The Devil's Ridge on the classic Ring of Steall. Turn left along the ridge and follow it over little rocky pinnacles to the summit of **Sgurr a'Mhaim** at 1099m (GR: NN165667). Return along the Devil's Ridge, enjoying the views out across the superb Mamores ridge.

Once you reach the spot where you gained the ridge earlier turn to the south-east and climb to the summit of **Sgurr an Iubhair** at 1001m. This used to be a Munro but was taken off the list in the 1990s.

The ridge to the south-east narrows again, and leads to a col below the impressive cone of **Am Bodach**. Climb the ridge to the top at 1032m (GR: NN177651). Now turn to the north-east and follow a jagged crest down to a col below a little minor top. Continue over this bump, then down into another col before ascending **Stob Coire a'Chairn**. ◀ The top is marked by a cairn at 981m (GR: NN185660).

The main ridge peels off to the south-east from here, but you can take a short diversion northwards to bag **An Gearanach** if you wish. It is a Munro (982m) and you may as well do it for completeness!

From the top of Stob Coire a'Chairn head south-east down into a col, then follow the ridge up the other side to the summit of **Na Gruagaichean** at 1056m (GR: NN203652). The view northwards from here is of Aonach Beag, while to the north-east your next objective, **Binnein Mor**, looks superb. Head just north of east, following the obvious ridge until it takes up to the summit of an intermediate peak, then turn northwards to gain Binnein Mor's summit at 1130m (GR: NN212663).

There are three ridges running out to the north from the summit. The north-western one is by far the easiest of the three, and you might want to follow that down until you are able to skirt eastwards into the corrie holding a little lochan. From here go north-eastwards to the larger lochan below the south face of **Binnein Beag**. The route to the top is straightforward, and the views from the summit cairn at 943m (GR: NN222677) are impressive.

From here you can see the whole of the route on the north side of Glen Nevis, from Stob Ban at the eastern end of the Grey Corries, through to the Aonachs, Carn Mor Dearg, and Ben Nevis.

On The Devil's Ridge on Sgurr a'Mhaim

On the summit of Binnein Beag

It is tempting here to head north-east down into the glen, but there is one more Munro on this grand traverse that should not be missed, **Sgurr Eilde Mor**.

Walk south back to the lochan on the col, and on its southern shore you will pick up a path. Follow this south-eastwards across the head of Coire a'Bhinnein then up towards the northern tip of **Coire an Lochain** (GR: NN225656). Turn to the east and climb the west ridge of Sgurr Eilde Mor to its summit at 1010m (GR: NN231658).

Now follow the long north-east ridge down towards the distant Abhainn Rath. You'll need to cross over this river, and it is best done high up at the point where it curves around to the east as it gushes out of the corrie to the north of the glen. Camp here for the night or head eastwards to the bothy at Meanach.

DAY 2

From the bothy at Meanach head north into Coire na Cabaig, then begin ascending diagonally to the north-west to gain the Druim **Meall a'Bhuirich** on Stob Ban. This is the long south-west ridge of the mountain, and you should aim for the low point along its length, between the minor top of Meall a'Bhuirich and the main summit of **Stob Ban**. Turn right along the ridge and follow this to Stob Ban's summit at 977m (GR: NN267724). Now descend to the north-west, down to a col where a little lochan sits on the ridge.

The **Grey Corries** ridge now lies before you. Climb northwards up the steep slopes of **Stob Choire Claurigh** to the summit at 1177m (GR: NN263738). ▶

Follow it over **Stob a'Choire Leith** at 1105m, **Stob Coire Cath na Sine** at 1079m, **Caisteil** at 1106m, and on to **Stob Coire an Laoigh**, at 1116m (GR: NN240725). Now the ridge veers away to the north-west to the sharp top of **Stob Coire Easain** at 1080m, before turning back to the south-west to take you up the final Munro of the Grey Corries, **Sgurr Choinnich Mor**, at 1094m (GR: NN227714).

South-west from Sgurr Choinnich Mor there is the final peak of the range to cross – **Sgurr Choinnich Beag** at 963m – before you can start on the Aonachs. Drop down off the west ridge of Sgurr Choinnich Beag to a col at 731m, high above Coire Bhealaidh.

Climb westwards up the impressive Stob Coire Bhealaich face of **Aonach Beag**. You soon find yourself on a fine jagged ridge walking to the summit of **Stob Coire Bhealaich** at 1101m. Handrail along the rim of the cliffs to your right to the summit of Aonach Beag at 1234m (GR: NN197715).

A path now leads north-westwards down to a col and from there easy ground rises to the north, levelling out as you approach the summit of **Aonach Mor** at 1221m (GR: NN193729).

Return southwards for 800m then take a bearing to the west. This leads down via rough ground to another col at 830m (GR: NN187723), and from there it is a

Westwards the Grey Corries ridge curves away, climbing and dipping over a number of superb peaks.

Ben Nevis's summit slopes from the Mamores

direct ascent to the summit of **Carn Mor Dearg** at 1220m. There are some steep rocky bulges on the ridge up to the summit, but you can stay to the right of these to ease ascent. The summit is marked by a large cairn on the edge of the knife-edge ridge (GR: NN177722).

Turn southwards from the summit of Carn Mor Dearg, descending along this famous arête. This requires some grade 1 scrambling, but is never too difficult, even with a big pack on your back.

The ridge curves gradually around to the south-west, and drops to a stony col at the head of Coire Leis. Follow the rim of the crags on the right for a while, and then climb up steep, bouldery slopes to the north-west, gaining the **Ben Nevis** summit plateau. The summit is very obvious and is marked by a large cairn, and a shelter at 1334m (GR: NN167713).

The summit plateau of Ben Nevis is a difficult place to navigate around in bad visibility. The Harvey British Mountain Map to Ben Nevis is particularly useful here as it has a 1:15,000 scale map of the Ben Nevis summit area on the rear of the standard map.

To descend to the Red Burn path and Fort William, follow a Grid Bearing of 231° for 150m, and then a Grid Bearing of 282° until you hit the zigzags of the Red Burn path.

This takes you down in long, gradual zigzags to a crossing of the Red Burn (GR: NN147718), then onwards to a junction at a big cairn overlooking **Lochan Meall an t-Suidhe** (GR: NN147724). Turn left here, and follow the obvious path down into Glen Nevis. Lower down in the glen the path splits (GR: NN133720). Turn left for the Glen Nevis youth hostel and the end of a fine high-level walk.

ROUTE 18

Fort William to Dalwhinnie

Total Distance	65km
Daily Distances	Day 1 – 22km, Day 2 – 27km, Day 3 – 16km
Maps	OS Landranger sheets 42 (Glen Garry & Loch Rannoch), and 41 (Ben Nevis)
Starting Point	Fort William (GR: NN105742).
Finishing Point	Dalwhinnie, on the A9 (GR: NN634849)

Area Summary

Covering some of the best glen routes through the Central Highlands, including those through Glen Nevis, the northern fringes of Rannoch Moor, the Ben Alder Forest and the shores of Loch Ericht, this is a superb route.

Route Summary

Starting off through lovely wooded Glen Nevis the route keeps to the low ground throughout. It leads you eastwards through the wild country between the Grey Corries and the Mamores before covering the rough moorland miles to Loch Ossian. The way then goes over a high pass, the Bealach Dubh, before descending to Culra Bothy. It's then an easy route out to Dalwhinnie along the banks of Loch Ericht. This route is suitable for those with little backpacking experience. The walking is easy, and the navigation is never too taxing.

Tourist Information
Cameron Square, Fort William (tel 01397 703781); Grampian Road, Aviemore (tel 01479 810363).

The Steall Falls at the head of Glen Nevis

Accommodation and Supplies
Good options in Fort William, and a hostel in Glen Nevis (tel 08701 553255 Central Reservations, website www.syha.org.uk). At the end of the walk, the Inn at Dalwhinnie (tel 01528 522257, website www.theinndalwhinnie.com) is a good place to spend the night.

Overnight Options
Camp along the route, or use the bothies at Meanach (GR: NN266685) on the north side of the Abhainn Rath, or Culra in the Ben Alder Forest (GR: NN523762). The SYHA hostel at Loch Ossian (GR: NN371670) is another good option (contact as above).

Escape Routes
This route follows a low level course and is in itself the best way out in bad weather or an emergency. Having said that, the station at Corrour gives a good way out via the West Coast railway line.

DAY 1
Head east out of **Fort William**, taking the Glen Nevis road at the roundabout. Here you are following the West Highland Way, only in the reverse direction to the hoards who do this long-distance trail.

At the visitor centre there's a path signposted to the west, and follow this up into the forest and onto a good track. Turn left and walk along the track, still on the West Highland Way, for 500m to a junction. Here the West Highland Way goes right, but you should continue straight ahead, taking the lower path up the glen.

Continue for 4km from the track junction, until you emerge from the plantation and onto the minor road that heads up the glen. Turn right along the road to a bridge, and instead of following the bridge over the road take a path on the right, following the **River Nevis** along its south bank towards the head of the glen. After 1.4km you will see a footbridge on the left going over the river, and it is best to take this (you can continue on the south side of the river, but the going gets very rough, and the path vanishes from time to time).

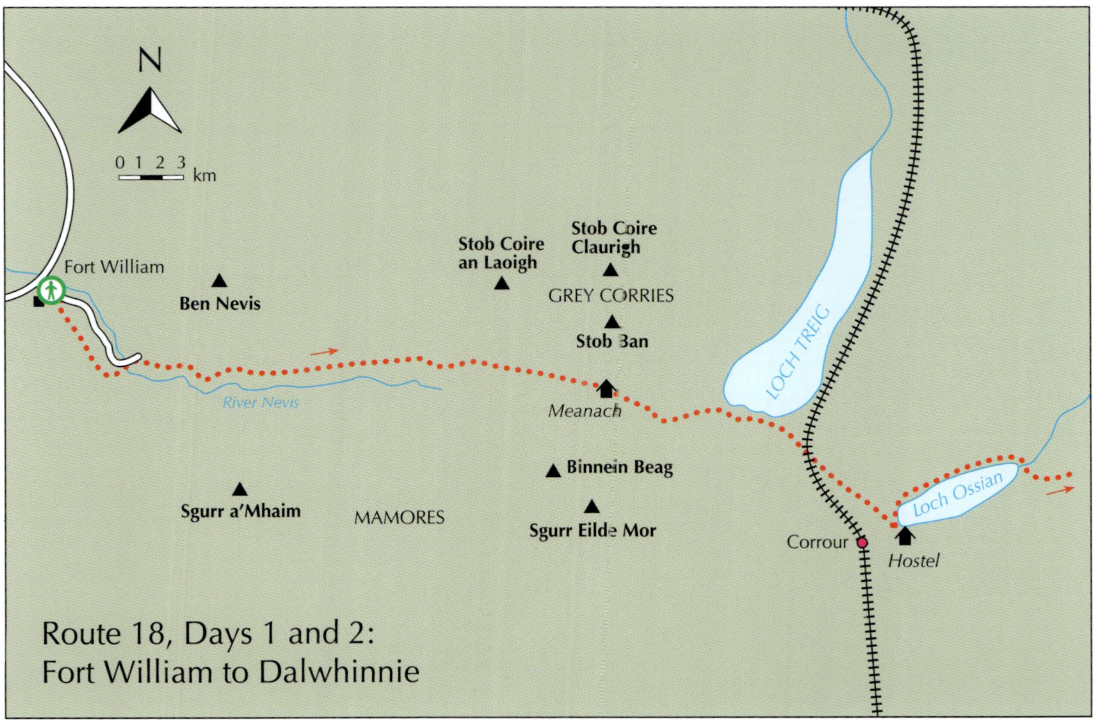

N
0 1 2 3 km
Fort William
Ben Nevis
River Nevis
Stob Coire an Laoigh
Stob Coire Claurigh
GREY CORRIES
Stob Ban
Meanach
LOCH TREIG
Binnein Beag
Sgurr a'Mhaim
MAMORES
Sgurr Eilde Mor
Corrour
Hostel
Loch Ossian
Route 18, Days 1 and 2:
Fort William to Dalwhinnie

The head of Glen Nevis

Turn right once over the bridge and follow the road to the car park at the head of the glen. At the back of the car park a path continues, and you should follow this in a big curve high above the **Nevis Gorge** until you emerge at a flat, grassy meadow below the wonderful Steall Falls.

There is a little white Climbers' Club hut on the opposite side of the river, with a wire bridge leading to the other side, but don't panic! You don't need to cross the bridge.

Walk eastwards along the north side of the infant river, passing the ruins at Steall, and continuing as the glen opens out. Towards the head of the Water of Nevis the path begins to get less and less obvious, but if you keep to the north side you are doing fine. Eventually you come to the end, or rather the start, of the River Nevis. A little boggy ground lies ahead and you should follow the vague path eastwards to the Abhainn Rath. Cross this river and pick up the path on its north side, following it for 2.6km to the bothy at **Meanach**.

DAY 2

Continue eastwards from the bothy at Meanach, following the Abhainn Rath all the way to the point where it is just about to enter **Loch Treig** (GR: NN309689). Here there is a bridge over the river, just before Creaguaineach Lodge. Walk over the bridge and follow a track heading generally east around the southern side of Loch Treig. Cross two more rivers via footbridges, then climb up on the track towards the West Highland railway line. The track follows the railway line for a short while, curving to the east. At the point where the railway swings away to the south-east, where the Allt Luib Ruairidh comes down from Beinn na Lap, the track ducks beneath the railway. Follow this and continue just south of east to the western side of **Loch Ossian**.

There is a track that circles Loch Ossian, and you can walk around it either way. However, on this route I would go on the north side of the loch. Turn left once you hit the track (turning right would take you to Loch Ossian hostel), and follow it to the north-eastern point of the loch. Here, at **Corrour Shooting Lodge** there is a big glen coming down from the east, and this has a path up the north side of the stream that issues from it. When you get to Corrour Shooting Lodge turn left to the edge of the wood, then right to pick up a footbridge leading over to this path. Follow the path eastwards up the Uisge Labhair.

Towards the head of the glen the path fades and you'll need to pick your own route to the obvious notch in the skyline above. The going is not too difficult and you'll soon find yourself crossing the deep col of **Bealach Dubh** (GR: NN481732).

Here you will pick up a path that leads down the other side.

Initially the way lies down a narrow corrie, and the scenery is superb, then as the corrie begins to open out lower down you get ever more amazing views of the mountains on either side, with Ben Alder to the south and Carn Dearg to the north.

The path runs along the north side of the stream, the Allt a'Bhealaich Dhuibh, and you should stay on this side all the way down to **Culra** bothy.

DAY 3

Just east of **Culra** bothy is a bridge and a path junction. Ignore the path going over the bridge and head just east of north along the main track. This takes you to the western end of lovely **Loch Pattack** where you'll come to another track junction. Turn right here, walking along the southern shore of Loch Pattack – you may have to wade across the river where it flows into the loch. Continue along the track until you reach another junction by a small plantation, and turn right here, following the track eastwards to **Ben Alder Lodge**.

At the lodge keep left until you are on the main track running north-eastwards along the shores of **Loch Ericht**. This is the main access route for those staying at Ben Alder Lodge, and a number of other, new buildings are now scattered along the shores of the loch. Continue along this track until you reach **Dalwhinnie** and the end of a fine walk.

The final day is in complete contrast to the previous two, as it takes you out of the mountains and onto the wooded lochside.

Beinn na Lap and Loch Ossian Youth Hostel tucked into the trees

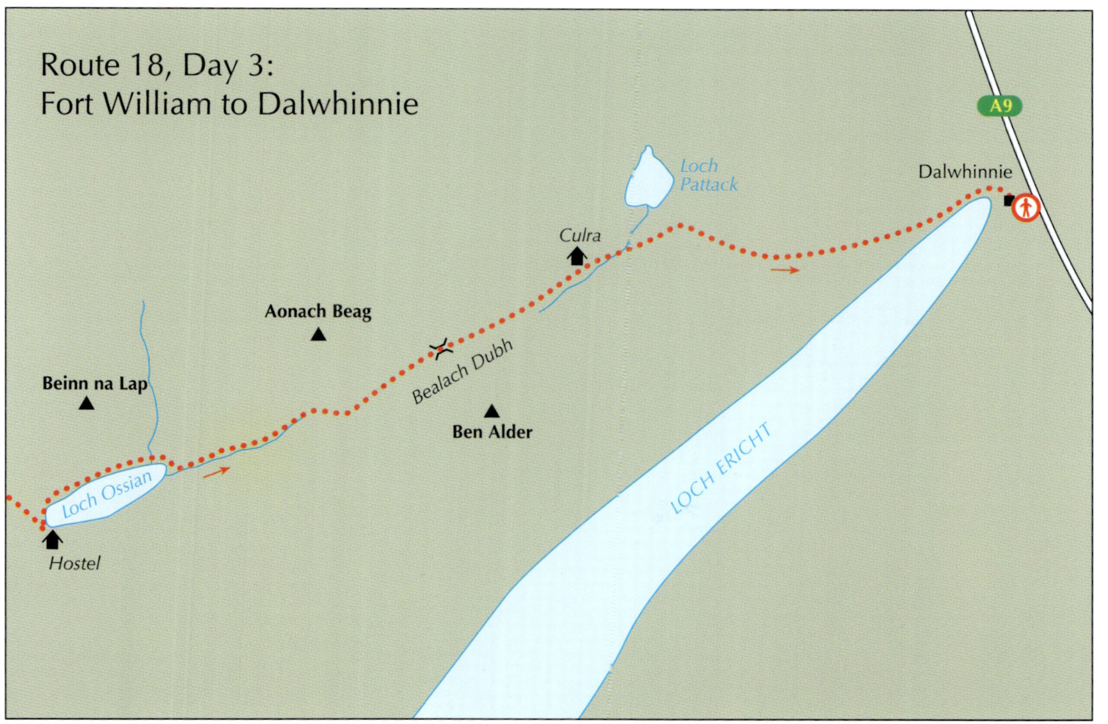

Route 18, Day 3:
Fort William to Dalwhinnie
A9
Loch Pattack
Dalwhinnie
Culra
Aonach Beag
Beinn na Lap
Bealach Dubh
Ben Alder
LOCH ERICHT
Loch Ossian
Hostel

ROUTE 19

Glen Coe from Appin

Total Distance	35km
Daily Distances	Day 1 – 18km, Day 2 – 17km
Maps	Harvey British Mountain Map 1:40,000 (Ben Nevis & Glen Coe)
Starting Point	Car par at the head of Glen Creran (GR: NN036488)

Area Summary

The hills to the south of the main Glen Coe Munros tend to be a bit ignored. Perhaps they suffer from being in such close proximity to the great mountains of the Aonach Eagach, Bidean nam Bian and the Buachailles. However, there are some lovely, wild corners to this part of Scotland, and while the mountains themselves provide a worthy challenge (see Route 27), the through routes are no less spectacular.

Route Summary

This route is hard considering that it's very much low level. The route takes you around some of the finest valley heads in the region, climbing over a number of passes between Munros, and traversing over a lot of rough ground to link together the three valleys of Glen Creran, Glen Etive, and Glen Coe. The route starts by heading east out of Glen Creran, going over a pass to the forested slopes of Glen Etive. You then traverse above the tree line, passing over a high col between Sgor na h-Ulaidh and Beinn Maol Chaluim. A descent down Fionn Ghleann then leads you to Glen Coe. The second day takes you over the lovely little peak of Sgorr a'Choise, before dropping you down into the forests at the head of Glen Creran. A wonderful, away-from-it-all kind of route.

Tourist Information
Cameron Square, Fort William (tel 01397 703781).

Accommodation and Supplies
Try the SYHA hostel in Glen Coe (tel 08701 553255 Central Reservations, website www.syha.org.uk), or camp at the Red Squirrel site just along the lane between the SYHA hostel and the Clachaig Inn.

Overnight Options
Camp in Glen Coe at the Red Squirrel site (as above), or stay in the Glen Coe hostel. The Clachaig Inn also has rooms (tel 01855 811252). You could even stay in either location the night before you start the walk, and leave your belongings in place so you can do the route without a big pack.

Escape Routes
The main continuation of Glen Creran offers an easy route through the mountains and down into Glen Coe. Glen Etive provides another possible escape route, although there are only a few farms in the glen, and the place can seem very deserted at times.

DAY 1
From the car park at the head of **Glen Creran** take the lane eastwards, passing the few houses at **Elleric**. The lane becomes a track behind the farm at Glenure, and you should bear right, down to the river where you'll find a bridge. Cross to the south side of the **River Ure** and turn eastwards, climbing up the narrow valley for 1.3km, until you see a footbridge leading back over to the north side of the river, 200m below the track. Drop down to the bridge and cross over again, then turn right and continue up the broad western slopes of An Grianan, moving northwards into the side valley holding the Allt Bealach na h-Innsig. The path drops down to cross the stream, then passes between it and a small lochan before fizzling out altogether. Continue up this narrow corrie to a col high on the southern slopes of **Beinn Fhionnlaidh**.

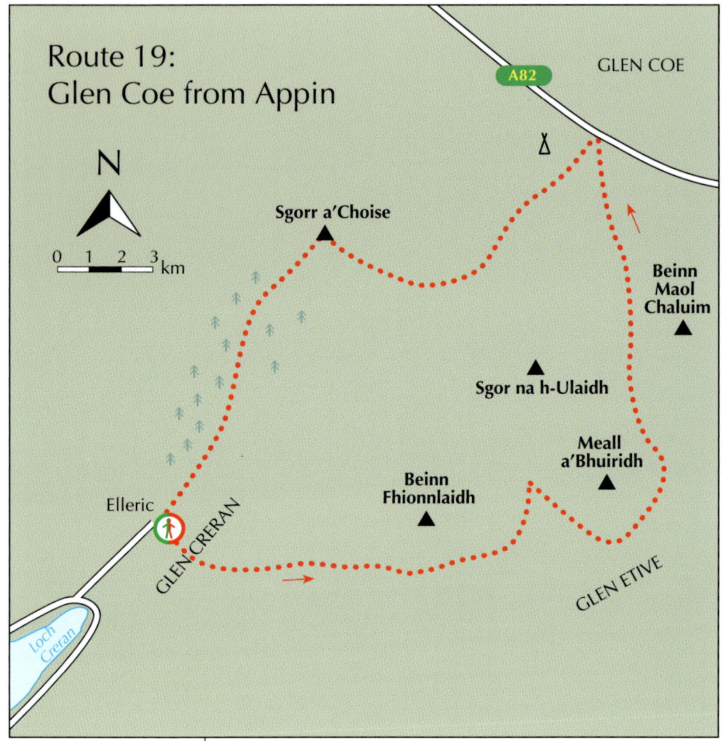

Descend from the col to the east, dropping down towards the vast forestry plantations that cloak the sides of Glen Etive below.

Do not continue all the way to the edge of the forest however, as your route now traverses the sides of the mountains to the north-east. Pass beneath **Meall nan Gobhar**, over rough ground, and then walk north-east to the head of a corrie below **Sgor na h-Ulaidh**. Contour south-eastwards, well below the Munro's south-east ridge, then after 2km veer northwards below the outlying minor top of **Meall Bhuiridh** and 100m or so above the forest line (GR: NN133502). Contour northwards below a belt

Looking up Glen Creran from the loch

of crags and up into the higher corrie from which the Allt Chaman issues. Now follow the stream to the north-west, keeping to its eastern side, until you are directly below the **Bealach Fhionnghaill** (GR: NN130516). Above you, blocking direct access to the bealach, is a craggy area, which you need to climb around to get to the col. Climb north-westwards until you are above the level of the crag, then move back to the north-east to gain the col. You are now between the Munro **Sgor na h-Ulaidh**, and the Munro **Beinn Maol Chaluim**.

The descent on the north side of the Bealach Fhionnghaill is straightforward, although the corrie you are heading down, **Fionn Ghleann**, is steep sided. Follow the stream all the way down to the main road, the A82, in Glen Coe. Turn right for the Clachaig Inn, the Red Squirrel Campsite, and the youth hostel, or turn left for the National Trust for Scotland campsite.

DAY 2

Back at the same point where you hit the A82 at the bottom of Fionn Ghleann yesterday, you'll notice another big glen cutting up to the south-west. Start by heading up the west side of the river to where these two glens meet (GR: NN118558). There's a track up the glen here and you can follow it until it drops down to cross the river. Stay on the north side of the river, the Allt na Muidhe, and follow it to the south-west until you reach the top of the glen and a col (GR: NN093542).

Turn to the north-west and climb to the right of the edge of a forest plantation, keeping to the open hill, until you reach the minor top of Meall a'Bhuige. This lies on the south-east ridge of **Sgorr a'Chois**e. Turn to the north-west and follow the broad ridge to the summit of this fine Graham (a mountain in Scotland between 2000 and 2500 feet) with a 150m drop on all sides. ◄

Descend the long south-west ridge of Sgorr a'Choise, passing over a little knoll at a spot height of 407m. Beyond this knoll, drop into a col, then climb out the other side, while still remaining on the ridge. Continue 500m from the col, until a path cuts diagonally

The top is a superb viewpoint for the main peaks of Glen Coe, and has a cairn at the highest point at 663m (GR: NN085551).

over the ridge, and here you should turn left, descending into the forests until you meet a big track cutting down **Glen Creran**. Turn right along this track and follow it down Glen Creran. Once you are down in the valley bottom the trees turn from conifers to broadleaved, mainly birch and oak, and here (GR: NN062521) you will come to a junction. Bear right and follow the track through the trees back to the car park.

Buachaille Etive Mor far above Loch Etive

ROUTE 20

Mull's Wilderness Coast

Total Distance	28km
Daily Distances	Day 1 – 16km, Day 2 – 12km
Maps	Ordnance Survey Explorer sheet no 375 (Isle of Mull, East)
Starting Point	On the north shore of Loch Scridain in a National Trust for Scotland car park (GR: NM477275).

Area Summary

The island of Mull lies off the western seaboard. To its east the waterway of the Firth of Lorn comes down from Loch Linnhe, while to the north the Sound of Mull separates the island from the wild lands of Morvern. To the west of Mull the Treshnish Isles, along with Tiree and Coll are set like jewels in the sea, while southwards Colonsay, Jura and Islay fill the horizon. This route tackles the remote headland known as the Wilderness – the western point of the Ardmeanach peninsula.

Route Summary

Although short, this is a rough and hard route into very remote country. It is a route for the experienced hillwalker, although it is regarded as an absolute classic. Some of the sections of the coastal route are only passable at low tide, and it is not always possible to escape upwards, so be prepared, and use common sense. The route follows the coast of the Ardmeanach Peninsula in a clockwise direction, returning over the rough hills of Beinn na h-Iolaire, Beinn na Sreine, and Maol Mheadhonach.

Tourist Information
The tourist office (tel 01680 812337) at Craignure shares the same building as the Calmac Office. For ferries contact Calmac (tel 08000 665000, website www.calmac.co.uk).

Accommodation and Supplies
Craignure is the arrival point for most people – the Oban ferry comes in here. The TIC in Craignure can advise on accommodation, or you could book into the Craignure Inn (tel 01680 812305). You can also camp at the Shieling Holidays Campsite in Craignure (tel 01680 812496, website www.shielingholidays.co.uk).

Overnight Options
Camp discreetly on the Ardmeanach peninsula. The owners of the farm at Balmeanach are not keen to encourage camping near the farm, so it is best to pitch up long before then, or else wait until you have passed through the farm and then camp wild In the hills.

Escape Routes
The only escape options from this route are to return the way you've come, or push on! Most parts of the coastal section are inescapable because of the high cliffs that fringe the coast, and only once you've reached the farm at Balmeanach can you hope to leave the route. You have been warned!

DAY 1

Although this route is superb if done as a two-day walk, camping wild along the way, the fit hillwalker may want to tackle it in a single day. As the return over the hills runs parallel to a minor road, it may be possible to shorten the walk, if you can arrange a car at each end.

On the north side of **Loch Scridain** the road runs along the shore for a while, then cuts northwards over the island, cutting off the Ardmeanach peninsula. Where it heads north you can park on the left down a dead-end lane. A track takes you westwards, a way above the

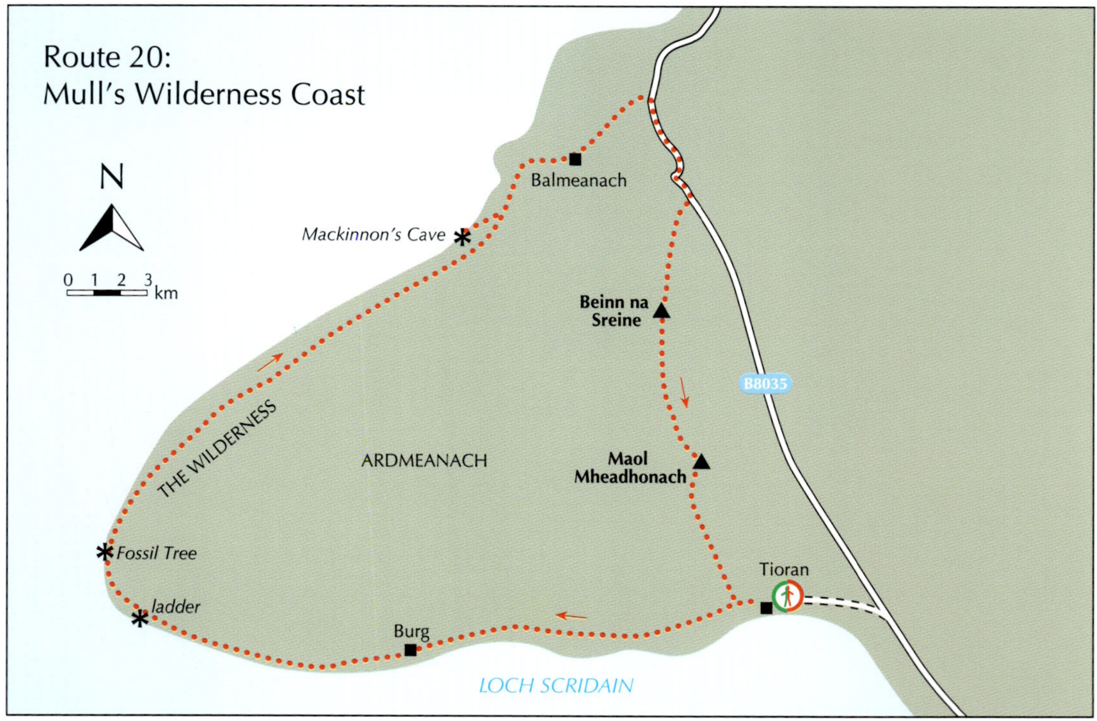

Route 20:
Mull's Wilderness Coast
N
0 1 2 3 km
Balmeanach
Mackinnon's Cave
Beinn na Sreine
B8035
Maol Mheadhonach
THE WILDERNESS
ARDMEANACH
Fossil Tree
ladder
Burg
Tioran
LOCH SCRIDAIN

shore. Ignore the path going off to the left to Scobull, and continue to the old Iron age fort at Dun Scobuill. The track continues westwards out of the woodlands, passing beneath the crags of Cnocan Donnchaidh, then onwards to **Tavool House**.

At Tavool House ignore the track that heads down to the shore, and continue south-westwards instead, to the farm at **Burg**. Walk beyond the farm, then down to the shore above Dun Bhuirg. ▶

Initially the going is quite straightforward, then as you get further and further around the headland you begin to realise just how remote and cut off you are.

A number of superb waterfalls cascade down the cliffs into the sea, and the path passes beneath these, sometimes just above the beach, sometimes on the shelves of raised beaches, left behind by lowering sea levels from hundreds of thousands of years ago. At one point, just beyond the rocky terraces of Carrachan Mor, you come to a steel ladder which you need to descend to gain access to the shore. A short way north of this, just past Uamh nan Eas, or the Cave of the Waterfall, you should look out for McCulloch's Fossil Tree, set in the rocks.

The Wilderness Coast of Mull's Ardmeanach Peninsula

The path passes beneath huge cliffs and raised beaches where white-tailed eagles soar overhead, while otters hunt for food down on the rocky shore.

There's much more excitement to come though. As you round the headland and begin the walk towards the mouth of **Loch na Keal**, passing through **The Wilderness**, you are approaching a huge gulf cut into the cliffs. This is the spectacular **Sloc nam Ban**, a vicious sea cleft, and one that you must climb up and around, as it is impassable and dangerous for the walker. Scramble 150 metres up the hill – above the rocky skerry of Sgeir na Faoilinn being about the best place to do this – then continue north-eastwards along the cliff tops. ◄

The cliff tops here make for a superb wild camp, with great views across to the Treshnish Isles and Staffa.

DAY 2

The route continues north-eastwards above the cliffs, and as you begin to approach the farm at **Balmeanach** you are passing above a spectacular sea cave. A path leads down to the beach from the cliff top near **Uamh Beathaig** (GR: NM442326) and you can double back by climbing down onto the shore, and at low tide, picking out a route to **Mackinnon's Cave**, the deepest cave in the Hebrides. ◄ When you've finished exploring Mackinnon's Cave return to the cliff top, then continue on a way-marked path to Balmeanach Farm.

Take a torch and explore the interior of the cave, but make sure the tide is still going out when you arrive.

From near Balmeanach the road cuts south over the high ground to Loch Scridain. The route on from here is fine though very rough. Follow the road south-eastwards to the point where it reaches the top of the hill (GR: NM454328) then walk southwards over rough ground to gain the ridge over **Beinn na h-Iolaire**. The ground to the east of this ridge falls away dramatically to the moor and forests overlooking the minor road, and you can handrail along this to **Beinn na Sreine** (GR: NM457304), and on to **Maol Mheadhonach**. The terrain here is rocky and there are countless little knolls and bluffs, but if you walk southwards to **Gib Bheinn** (GR: NM461285) you can descend alongside to the south east to the hidden Loch Arish, then pick a careful route down beside the Allt an Sgaphair to Dun Scobuill, and so back to the car park.

Mull is one of the best places in Scotland to view white-tailed eagles. These huge birds of prey – even bigger

Exploring Mackinnon's Cave

than the golden eagle, with a wingspan of over eight feet – were extinct in Scotland by 1917. Then in the 1970's the NCC began to reintroduce birds from Norway, and over 140 birds have since been brought over. The first British chick was successfully reared by a wild pair on Rum in 1985. The numbers have steadily risen, and they are regularly seen flying throughout the island.

ROUTE 21

The Black Mount

Total Distance	48km
Daily Distances	Day 1 – 19km, Day 2 – 18km, Day 3 – 11km
Maps	OS Landranger sheet 50 (Glen Orchy)
Starting Point	Victoria Bridge (GR: NN271422) at the western end of Loch Tulla, just beyond the Inveroran Hotel.

Area Summary

The Black Mount is a superb range for the backpacker to explore. The best features of the range are hidden from the road, and so you need to get up into the high corries and onto the tops to see these. There is a wealth of great routes into and through these mountains – this route covers what I consider to be the best. This is a high level route, but the lower level options would also be worth a visit.

Route Summary

The route traverses seven of the Munros of the Black Mount, starting at Victoria Bridge. The final summit, Ben Starav, is a brilliant viewpoint, with the whole of Loch Etive stretching away to the south-west. This is a real connoisseur's route, and you'll want to return to this area of the Highlands time and time again.

Tourist Information

The nearest TIC is in Tyndrum just south of Bridge of Orchy (tel 01838 400246).

Accommodation and Supplies

The Inveroran Hotel (tel 01838 400220, website www.inveroran.com) is very close to the start, while the Bridge of Orchy Hotel (tel 01838 400208, website www.bridgeoforchy.co.uk) is also nearby and has a bunkhouse. There are plenty of shops in Tyndrum, as well as good places to stay.

Overnight Options
Camp wild along the route.

Escape Routes
The best escape routes are via Glen Kinglass. Head south from any point along the ridge route and you'll find yourself either in Glen Kinglass itself, or further east along the Abhainn Shira. Head east along these glens to reach Victoria Bridge.

DAY 1

Start by crossing to the north side of **Victoria Bridge**. There's a junction immediately ahead at Forest Lodge, and you should turn left, alongside the **Abhainn Shira**. Follow the track for 1.6km to the point where the Allt Toaig comes down from the corrie to the north. The main track crosses the burn, whereas the path you want heads north along-side the Allt Toaig, and up into the wild Coire Toaig. The path keeps to the east side of the Allt Toaig, and you'll notice a wide gully cutting down from the col that lies between **Beinn Toaig** and **Stob a'Choire Odhair** to the north-east. The path climbs above the Allt Toaig to cross the side stream that comes down this gully (GR: NN253446). Cross over, then take a path that climbs steeply up the south face of Stob a'Choire Odhair, ascending right to the summit at 947m (GR: NN257460).

Turn westwards and descend the west ridge to a col at the head of Coire Toaig. Climb westwards from the col for 500m, then turn to the south-west up steep slopes and scree to gain an arête known as the Aonach Eagach (no, not the famous ridge by the same name – that's further north in Glen Coe!). Turn westwards again along this ridge, follow a path along the crest to the summit of **Stob Ghabhar** at 1087m (GR: NN230455).

Descend the west ridge from the summit, dropping to a col before climbing over a subsidiary bump. Here

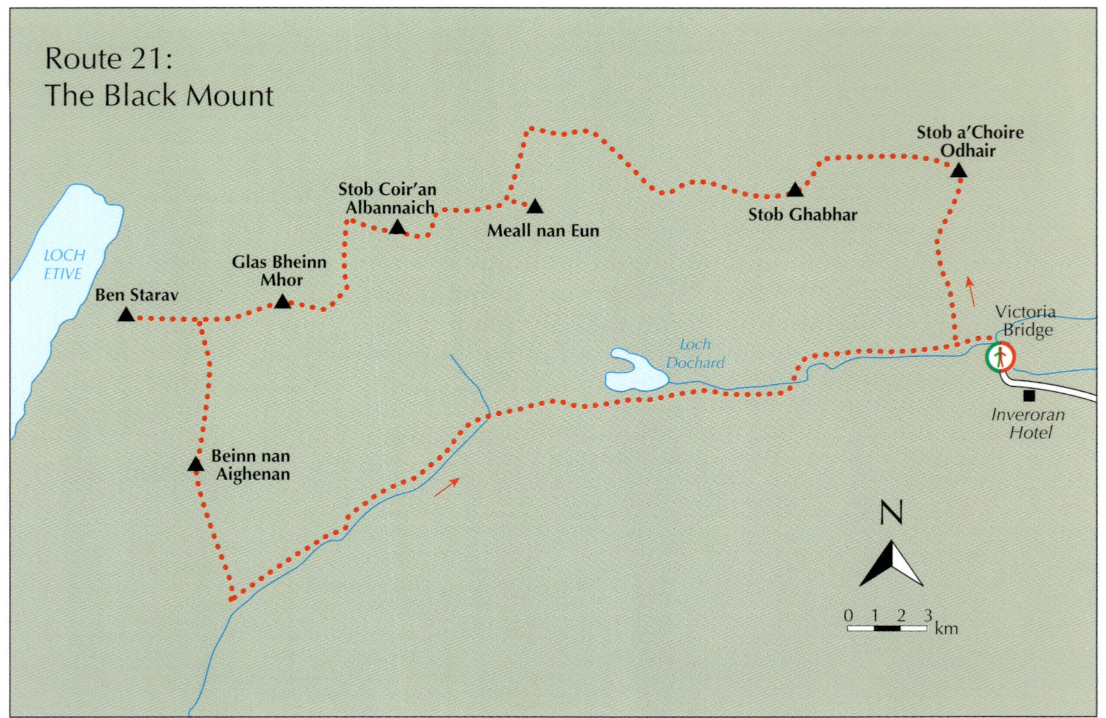

Route 21:
The Black Mount
Stob a'Choire Odhair
Stob Ghabhar
Stob Coir'an Albannaich
Meall nan Eun
Glas Bheinn Mhor
Ben Starav
Beinn nan Aighenan
LOCH ETIVE
Loch Dochard
Victoria Bridge
Inveroran Hotel
N
0 1 2 3 km

the main ridge sweeps around to the north, but you should leave this and follow a bearing down to the Bealach Coire Laoghan (GR: NN214457). Climb out of the other side of this col, over **Stob a'Bhruaich Leith** at 941m, then north-westwards to another minor bump, known as Fair Bhan. Here the ridge swings to the west, and you should continue along this to **Meall Odhar** at 876m (GR: NN190465).

Now descend steep slopes to the south, gaining a col at the head of Coire nan Cmamh. A steep climb up to the south brings you out onto the broad north-west ridge of **Meall nan Eun**, your third Munro of the day. Turn south-eastwards and climb the ridge to the summit at 928m (GR: NN193449).

Return along the north-west ridge for 500m, then descend to the south-west, to a col before the knoll of **Meall Tarsuinn**. Climb up to the top of Meall Tarsuinn at 875m, then down the opposite side to a col (GR: NN174445) above the **Allt Coire Chaorach**. You may well have had enough for the day, so could look for somewhere to camp in this vicinity.

DAY 2

Immediately above the col upon which you've camped lies the first Munro of the day, **Stob Coir'an Albannaich**. The easiest ascent is to head south until you gain the east ridge of the mountain. The going is rough but you'll soon be standing on the crest. Turn along the ridge and climb it easily to the summit at 1044m (GR: NN169443).

Take a bearing to the south-west, aiming for the top of **Sron nan Cabar** where two streams on either side of the ridge are only 200m apart. Once between the two streams walk south-east down the ridge of Sron nan Cabar for 300m, then bear south-west down to a col. Climb up to the south-west, along the north-east ridge of **Glas Bheinn Mhor**. This north-east ridge is a spur of the east ridge of the mountain, and once on this main ridge you can turn west and walk up the narrow arête to the top at 993m (GR: NN154429).

The Black Mount in winter

One more Munro awaits, way over to the west, while another lies to the south. To reach the western Munro, **Ben Starav**, involves a switch-back ridge. Head south-west from the summit of Glas Bheinn Mhor, down to a col, then westwards to the little cone of Meall nan Tri Tighearnan. From the top a ridge runs to the south-west for 500m, ending in a spur (GR: NN142423), then curves around to the north-west and down to another col. Follow this ridge, then continue up the other side from the col, gaining the minor top of Stob Coire Dheirg, which is the eastern summit of Ben Starav. A rocky arête leads off to the south-west, and from there it is an easy walk to the north-west to reach the top of Ben Starav at 1078m (GR: NN126427).

Return along the ridge as far as the spur (GR: NN142423) on Meall nan Tri Tighearnan. Now drop down to the south, to a low col at the head of **Coire na Caime**.

A steep climb to the south-east leads up to the fine summit of **Beinn nan Aighenan** at 957m (GR: NN148404), the final Munro of the route.

Descend into **Glen Kinglass** to the south by heading south-west down the ridge enclosing Coire Coinnich on its west side. This leads down to a flat area on the ridge, with a knoll in its middle at 750m. Here turn just to the east of south and descend along the side of Eas an Eich Bhain, with the burn running to your left. You'll hit a path lower down that takes you down to the track in the bottom of Glen Kinglass. Turn left along the track, passing by Glenkinglass Lodge on the other side of the river.

Continue along the River Kinglass, heading north-east until you get to a bridge over the river at **Innseag na h-Iuraiche**. ▶

The confluence of two rivers is just upstream, and if you cross the bridge and follow the path up into Coire Beithe you will find some lovely camping spots.

DAY 3

Return to the path and continue north-eastwards, heading for the southern shore of **Loch Dochard**. Follow the path along the south side of the loch, then along the Abhainn Shira until you reach a bridge on the left (GR: NN233418). Cross here to the north side, and follow the path that just skirts the plantation before heading eastwards to pick up a track coming down from the farm at **Clashgour**. Stay on the south side of the forestry plantation, between it and the river, and continue through to Forest Lodge and your car at **Victoria Bridge**.

ROUTE 22
Across Rannoch Moor

Total Distance	34km
Daily Distances	Day 1 – 21km, Day 2 – 13km
Maps	Harvey British Mountain Map 1:40,000 (Ben Nevis & Glen Coe)
Starting Point	Corrour station, on the line between Glasgow and Fort William (GR: NN355664)

Area Summary

This is a little-visited group of hills on the northern fringes of Rannoch Moor, benefiting from the easy access provided by the West Highland Railway Line. There are countless opportunities for exploration within this wilderness region, including ascents of some lesser hills.

Route Summary

The route heads north from Corrour station to Loch Treig from where you head west to Staoineag. The long north ridge of Glas Bheinn (Corbett) is ascended, then a route is taken to the east over to Beinn na Cloiche. The bothy at Loch Chiarain makes a good place to spend the night. On day two Leum Uilleim is traversed on the route back to Corrour Station.

Tourist Information

Cameron Square, Fort William (tel 01397 703781).

Accommodation and Supplies

There are plenty of options in Fort William. The SYHA hostel at Loch Ossian (GR: NN371670) is just east of Corrour station (tel 08701 553255 Central Reservations, website www.syha.org.uk).

Overnight Options
Camp along the route, or use the bothy at Loch Chiarain (GR: NN289634).

Escape Routes
Head back to Corrour station for the easiest escape routes in bad weather.

DAY 1

From **Corrour station** do not cross to the east side of the line. There is a path that heads north on the west side of the tracks, and you should follow this. Soon the path becomes more of a track and you should follow this to the southern shore of **Loch Treig** where a bridge takes you over the Abhainn Chamabreac (GR: NN327690). Continue westwards along the track to a bridge over the Allt Iolairean at Lochtreighead, then continue to the outflow of the **Abhainn Rath** where a bridge goes over to Creaguaineach Lodge. Don't cross over the Abhainn Rath, but turn south-westwards with the river to your right. In 2km you'll come to the little bothy at **Staoineag**. Beyond here, but still going westwards on the south side

Creaguaineach Lodge at the head of Loch Treig

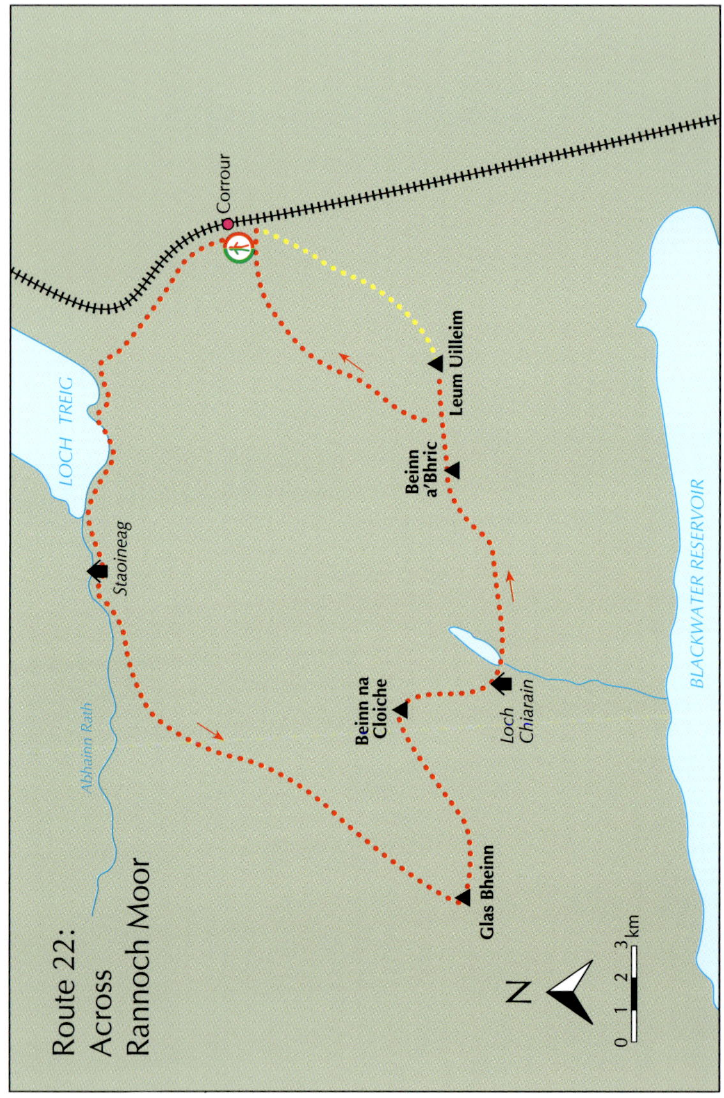
Corrour
Leum Uilleim
Beinn a'Bhric
Staoineag
LOCH TREIG
Abhainn Rath
Beinn na Cloiche
Loch Chiarain
Glas Bheinn
BLACKWATER RESERVOIR
Route 22:
Across
Rannoch Moor
N
0 1 2 3 km

of the Abhainn Rath, the path is vague at the best of times. However, with the river to act as a guide you really can't go wrong. Cross the Allt Gleann na Giubhsachan, 1km from Staoineag, then continue for 500m more alongside the Abhainn Rath. Now walk south-westwards, climbing onto the ridge known as Ceann Caol na Glas-bheinne. This ridge leads all the way to the summit of **Glas Bheinn**. Just keep going to the south-west, and you will eventually reach the summit of this fine Corbett at 792m (GR: NN258641).

From the summit you get a good view of your next objective, **Beinn na Cloiche**, away to the north-east. Eastwards the view is dominated by the bulky slopes of **Leum Uilleim**, your Corbett for tomorrow.

To get to **Beinn na Cloiche** you must first head south for 1km – there's a lot of steep scree to cross if you try to go directly towards Beinn na Cloiche from the summit of Glas Bheinn. On the south ridge of Glas Bheinn you'll come to a knoll and a tiny lochan, and from there you can turn to the north-east, aiming for the southern tip of **Lochan Tom Ailein** (GR: NN271639). ▶

From the lochan head due east up onto the south-west ridge of Beinn na Cloiche. You should hit the broad ridge just above a tiny lochan (GR: NN278639). From here turn to the north-east and climb easy slopes to the summit at 646m (GR: NN284648).

Descend to the south for 1.5km over gentle but hummocky ground, then veer off to the east to the southern end of **Loch Chiarain**, to the bothy that lies just back from the water's edge.

DAY 2

Start the day by carefully crossing the Chiaran Water, the river that issues from the southern end of **Loch Chiarain**.

Once on the ridge above Leac nan Carn, turn to the north and handrail around onto the vast plateau area. Make first for the subsidiary top of **Beinn a'Bhric** at 876m (GR: NN317643), then descend slightly to the col

This lochan is an oddity in that it seems to drain away at both ends.

Head eastwards up the broad flanks of Leum Uilleim, onto the ridge overlooking the massive southern corrie.

175

Leum Uilleim from Corrour Station

to its east. From there it is an easy ascent to the summit of **Leum Uilleim** at 909m. It's a shame that this mountain isn't just that bit higher. Another 5.4m and Leum Uilleim would be a Munro! Perhaps it's better for being a 'lowly' Corbett though, as it relatively unknown and untrodden. There are two ways down to the station at Corrour that you can now see down on the moor to the north-east.

For a short return simply head north-east from the summit, picking up a superb ridge route that forms the southern arm of the magnificent corrie, **Coir'a'Bhric Beag**. This ridge, **Sron an Lagain Ghairbh**, leads easily down onto the moor, and you can then forge a way across the heathery ground to reach **Corrour**.

A slightly longer route takes the ridge to the north of Coir' a'Bhric Beag. Head west back to the col at 800m, then turn northwards to pick up the ridge down to **Tom an Eoin**. This ridge has a path down its length leading onto the moor and back to Corrour.

ROUTE 23
The Crianlarich Munros

Total Distance	37km
Daily Distances	Day 1 – 21km, Day 2 – 16km
Maps	OS Landranger sheets 50 (Glen Orchy), 51 (Loch Tay), & 56 (Loch Lomond)
Starting Point	Crianlarich (GR: NN384251)

Area Summary

A magnificently varied region of open glens and wooded hillsides, with a broad scattering of Munros and Corbetts nearby. The two main roads to the Western Highlands, the A82 and the A85, meet at Crianlarich, effectively cutting off the mountains to the south of Crianlarich from the other ranges close by.

Route Summary

The route begins by following the route of the West Highland Way, going southwards. There is then a steep climb onto the western end of a long and rough ridge containing seven Munros, and a high camp is taken on this traverse. A surprisingly tough route, requiring good navigational ability.

Tourist Information

The nearest TICs are in Killin (tel 01567 820254) and Tyndrum (tel 01838 400246).

Accommodation and Supplies

There are a few options in Crianlarich for accommodation, including the SYHA hostel (tel 01838 300260, website www.syha.org.uk).

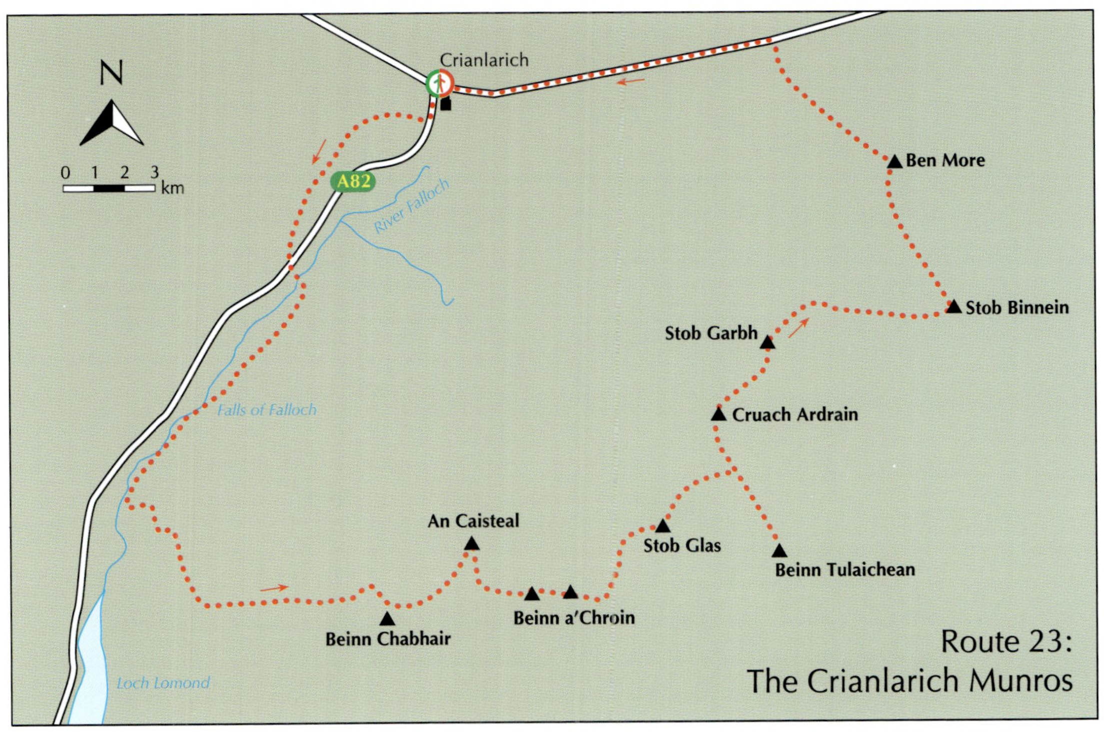
Crianlarich
N
0 1 2 3 km
A82
River Falloch
Falls of Falloch
Loch Lomond
Ben More
Stob Binnein
Stob Garbh
Cruach Ardrain
An Caisteal
Stob Glas
Beinn Tulaichean
Beinn a'Chroin
Beinn Chabhair
Route 23:
The Crianlarich Munros

Overnight Options
Camp wild on the hill at any point that takes your fancy!

Escape Routes
All of the Munros have ridges running down to the north, towards Crianlarich, and these form the best means of escape in an emergency.

DAY 1

The first few kilometres of this route follows the West Highland Way southwards, and to get onto it from the road junction in the centre of **Crianlarich** you should make for the **railway station** and cross the A82 to its west side. Here you'll see a track cutting up westwards through the conifer plantation. Follow this to where it emerges from the trees. There's a track junction here, with the main route of the West Highland Way cutting across from south to north. Turn left, southwards, and follow the track alongside a line of electricity pylons. The track then dips beneath a 'sheep creep', a low tunnel under the A82. Go under this and down to the banks of the **River Falloch**. Turn south-westwards and continue alongside the river to the farm at **Derrydaroch**. Cross the river via the bridge at the farm, then continue downstream along the south side of the river. ◄ Continue beyond the falls for 1.5km, to a point just before the valley turns sharply to the south. here you'll spot a path zigzagging steeply up the hill to the south-east. Follow this path, climbing steadily to 300m, to a point just above the Beinglas Falls. Now turn eastwards, following the **Ben Glas Burn** up to its source at **Lochan Beinn Chabhair** (GR: NN355178).

Above the loch the corrie curves around to the south, ending at a col that lies between **Beinn Chabhair** and Parlan Hill. Walk up to this col, then turn eastwards up the rocky ridge of Creag Bhreac Mhor. Now climb steep slopes to the north-east, topping out on Beinn Chabhair at 931m (GR: NN367179). This is the first Munro of the traverse, but two more lie close by to the north-east.

Soon you'll reach the spectacular **Falls of Falloch**

To get to the first, **An Caisteal**, you need to descend rocky slopes to a col to the north-east. Now turn to the east and climb up to a higher col that lies between An Caisteal and **Beinn a'Chroin** (GR: NN382185). As you'll be returning to this col, you could leave your rucksack here if you wish. Turn north along the narrow ridge above the col and you soon find yourself on the superb summit of An Caisteal at 995m (GR: NN378193).

Return to the col, then climb eastwards along a path to the western top of Beinn a'Chroin. The eastern top, which is higher, and the summit of the Munro, lies 1km east and is crowned by a cairn at 940m (GR: NN394186).

You may well be thinking of finding a campsite soon. Perhaps the best option is to descend the north ridge of Beinn a'Chroin for 800m, to the top of a rocky spur, then to walk across the head of a small gully to the north-east to a flat area just below a col west of **Stob Glas** (GR: NN399197).

DAY 2

Climb north-east to the top of the little rocky knoll of Stob Glas, then continue to the north-east over an undulating ridge that connects this peak to **Cruach Ardrain**.

To the south-east of Cruach Ardrain and out on a spur lies another Munro, **Beinn Tulaichean**, and it makes sense to climb this before tackling Cruach Ardrain. From the ridge north-east of Stob Glas you should climb up to a knoll about midway between Stob Glas and Cruach Ardrain (GR: NN406205). Now turn to the east and traverse across to the ridge that connects the two Munros. You could leave your pack here to pick up on your return.

Walk to the south-east, down into a col, then up the other side to the summit of **Beinn Tulaichean** at 945m (GR: NN417196). Return via the same route to the col, and climb back onto the south-east ridge of Cruach Ardrain, continuing to the summit at 1045m (GR: NN408211).

Head north-east down the rocky ridge, continuing down steeper slopes below as you descend diagonally to the col at the head of Benmore Glen (GR: NN422226). The west face of **Stob Binnein** lies ahead, and you can climb straight up this to the summit at 1165m (GR: NN435227).

The way on to **Ben More** is now straightforward. Head north along the ridge from Stob Binnein's summit, dropping to the Bealach-eadar-dha Beinn, then continuing on grassy slopes to the summit of your final Munro, Ben More at 1174m (GR: NN433244).

To the north-west of the summit of Ben More is a great, scoured bowl in the hillside. This is very rough, but the slopes immediately to its east are easy and grassy for the most part.

Head in the direction of the western end of **Loch Iubhair** down in the glen, then veer off more towards **Ben More Farm** once you are lower down the hill. You will meet the A85 just to the east of the farm, and from there it is a short walk along the road back to Crianlarich.

ROUTE 24

Ben Vorlich from Glen Artney

Total Distance	33km
Daily Distances	Day 1 – 17km, Day 2 – 16km
Maps	OS Landranger sheet 57 (Stirling and the Trossachs)
Starting Point	The car park by the chapel at the head of Glen Artney (GR: NN711161)

Area Summary

A lovely region of high mountains flanked by quiet moorlands. The two Munros of this area, Ben Vorlich and Stuc a'Chroin, are popular hills but are usually climbed from the north near Lochearnhead. Other hills scattered around this glen include a number of remote Corbetts and Grahams.

Route Summary

The route circles the head of Glen Artney, starting by taking the walker into the quiet hills to the north of the glen. You first traverse Beinn Dearg and Meall na Fearna before coming to grips with the two Munros. On the second day, after a high camp by the stunning Lochan a'Chroin, the routes takes you over Beinn Eich before dropping you down right at the head of the glen. Good tracks then lead back east to the car park.

Tourist Information

The nearest TIC is in Crieff (tel 01764 652578).

Accommodation and Supplies

The best place to find somewhere to stay and to buy supplies for a walk is in Crieff. The TIC there is the place to go for information on B&Bs.

Overnight Options
Camp wild on the hill at any point that takes your fancy!

Escape Routes
Drop into Glen Artney from any point along the route.

DAY 1
From the car park you should begin by heading east along the lane. Cross the bridge and then take the first turning on the left, past Dalchruin Farm. Just beyond Dalchruin the track swings close to the river, and there is a bridge here that takes you over to Dalclathick. Take the track over the bridge, then bear right, and right again over a bridge crossing the Allt Glas. Once over this bridge there is another track, this time going off on the left, uphill. Follow this track around the back of a small wood, then climb up the east side of the Allt Glas until you are opposite a small quarry on the other side of the corrie (GR: NN712187).

Cross the Allt Glas and climb up to the south side of the small quarry, following a burn onto the southern flank of **Beinn Dearg**. Continue alongside the burn until you leave it behind high up on the hill. Continue northwards to the small summit plateau. The top lies over on the left (GR: NN697197).

There is a ridge running westwards for 100m, and you should follow this, continuing along it as it turns to the south-west and down to a continuation ridge with a number of knolls along its top. Drop into a col, then climb out the other side and continue to a spot height at **706m** (GR: NN685190).

Turn to the north-west and descend steeply to a gap between two small woods in the valley bottom. Here, down near the head of **Strath a'Ghlinne**, you will meet a track. Follow this down to the river, and cross over to the other bank immediately. Now climb westwards for 300m to pick up the bottom of a north-east facing ridge.

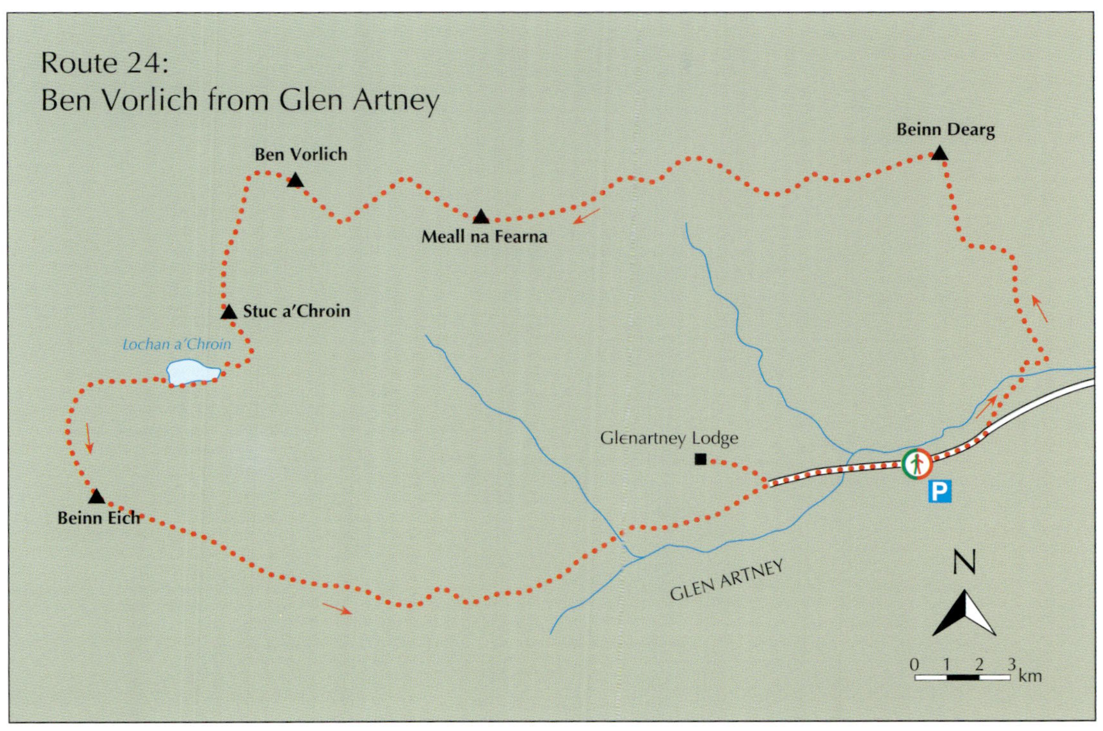
Route 24:
Ben Vorlich from Glen Artney
Beinn Dearg
Ben Vorlich
Meall na Fearna
Stuc a'Chroin
Lochan a'Chroin
Beinn Eich
Glenartney Lodge
GLEN ARTNEY
N
0 1 2 3 km
P

Climb this to the south-west, gaining a rocky little knoll above Coire na Cloiche. The ridge gets a bit broader above this knoll and leads you up to a spot height at 742m (GR: NN660190). The top of your first Corbett of the trip, **Meall na Fearna**, lies 1km away to the west, and it is an easy climb to its top from this spot height. The summit has a cairn at 809m (GR: NN651187).

Descend the broad and rough north-west ridge of Meall na Fearna to a subsidiary top (GR: NN644191). From here another ridge runs down to the south-west, to a col between Meall na Fearna and **Ben Vorlich**.

Descend to the col, then climb very steeply up to the south-west to gain the south-east ridge of Ben Vorlich. Turn right once on the ridge and follow it to the summit at 985m (GR: NN629189). The top is marked by an OS trig pillar and a cairn.

The views across to **Stuc a'Chroin** show how rough that Munro is, and to get there you must pick a careful route.

Descend from Ben Vorlich's summit to the west, then curve around on a path to the south-west to reach **Bealach an Dubh Choirein**. Clamber along the ridge, then follow a faint path around the east side of Stuc a'Chroin. The path is a bit vague at times, but it does lead you up onto the north ridge of Stuc a'Chroin. Turn to the south and continue to the summit at 972m (GR: NN617174). ◄

First head south-east along the summit ridge, descending for about 500m to a flattish area on the ridge. Now turn to the south-west and drop into the hanging valley to the lochan.

DAY 2

Start the day by descending diagonally westwards into the head of **Gleann a'Chroin**. Aim for a tiny lochan just below **Bealach nan Cabar**, and try to get there without descending too far into the corrie head, as you'll only have to climb out again!

From the lochan climb up to the bealach and turn south on the hummocky ridge to reach the summit of **Beinn Eich** at 811m (GR: NN603157).

There's a really good camp site just below the summit to the south, at **Lochan a'Chroin**.

There is a very long south-east ridge running off Beinn Eich into the head of Gleann a'Chroin. Follow this ridge over the subsidiary hill of **Meall na Caora**, then on to a short rise at the far end (GR: NN625140).

Drop down just south of east, aiming for the small **reservoir** just below Sgiath an Dobhrain. Make towards the northern tip of the reservoir and cross the inflowing stream so that you are on the east side. Now head east for the track at the old building at Arivurichardich. Once on the track you can follow it eastwards over a broad col and around the lower slopes of Tom Odhar to gain the headwaters of **Water of Ruchill** at a side stream. Cross this side stream, the Allt an Dubh Choirein, via a bridge, and turn right down the glen for a short way. The track then cuts eastwards over a gentle shoulder, known as **Monadh Odhar**, and down to the road head below **Glenartney Lodge**. Once on the road cross the Water of Ruchill via the bridge and walk down the lane back to your car.

The view from Ben Vorlich's summit

ROUTE 25

Ben Lawers and Meall nan Tarmachan

Total Distance	38km
Daily Distances	Day 1 – 20km, Day 2 – 18km
Maps	OS Landranger sheet 51 (Loch Tay)
Starting Point	Invervar, in Glen Lyon (GR: NN666483)

Area Summary

A surprisingly remote round of a group of very popular Munros. The Ben Lawers range is one of the most frequented groups of hills in Scotland, being within easy reach of day trippers from Glasgow and Edinburgh. Most of these day walkers simply bag the Munros from the National Trust for Scotland Visitor Centre, whereas this route tackles the wild northern side of the range, overlooking Glen Lyon. To the south of the range is the huge stretch of Loch Tay.

Route Summary

The route takes to these great tops from the north, starting with a walk up the glen from Invervar. The first summit is Meall a'Choire Leith, and for the time being the rest of the main tops of the Ben Lawers range are ignored as you head for the Corbett, Meall nan Maigheach. Southwards lies a long traverse to Meall nan Tarmachan, and a high camp on that mountain. Day two will take you along the superb Ben Lawers ridge, taking in all the remaining Munros before you descend to Glen Lyon and the end of the walk.

DAY 1

From the road in **Invervar** there are tracks going off to the north and south. Take the one to the south that drops down to the river at a bridge. Cross over and turn right, following a big track heading up the glen. Walk along

Tourist Information
The nearest TIC is in Killin (tel 01567 820254). The National Trust for Scotland also have an information centre (tel 01567 820397), just below the road pass that separates Ben Lawers from Meall nan Tarmachan.

Accommodation and Supplies
There are plenty of shops in Killin, as well as the usual B&B and hotel options. The SYHA Hostel is a good place to stay (tel 01567 820546, website www.syha.org.uk).

Overnight Options
Camp wild on Meall nan Tarmachan, or anywhere else you like the look of.

Escape Routes
Descend either into Glen Lyon, or southwards to the Loch Tay road. In an emergency the National Trust Visitor Centre (GR: NN608378) is a good place to get help, at least when it is open during the day.

this for 4.5km, passing the farm at Inverinain after 1.6km. Beyond **Roromore** you will come to a track junction at a stream. Here, turn south, follow the track uphill alongside the Allt a'Chobhair.

This track ends at a hut and a bunch of old shielings, and at this point you should cross the Allt a'Chobhair to its west side. Ahead lies the open Coire Ban, with broad ridges running down each enclosing side. Head west to gain the ridge with the corrie to its left. Once on the ridge you can head southwards towards the summit of **Meall a'Choire Leith**. The summit of this Munro is marked by a cairn at 926m (GR: NN613439).

Descend south-westwards into the wilds of Coire Gorm, then walk westwards across the flat upper reaches of **Gleann Da-Eig**. Continue westwards onto the broad, heathery south-east ridge of **Meall nan Maigheach**, then turn along its easy slopes and follow a faint path to the summit at 780m (GR: NN586436).

Return along the south-east ridge, continuing down to a col then over the rounded lump of **Meall na Eun**. On

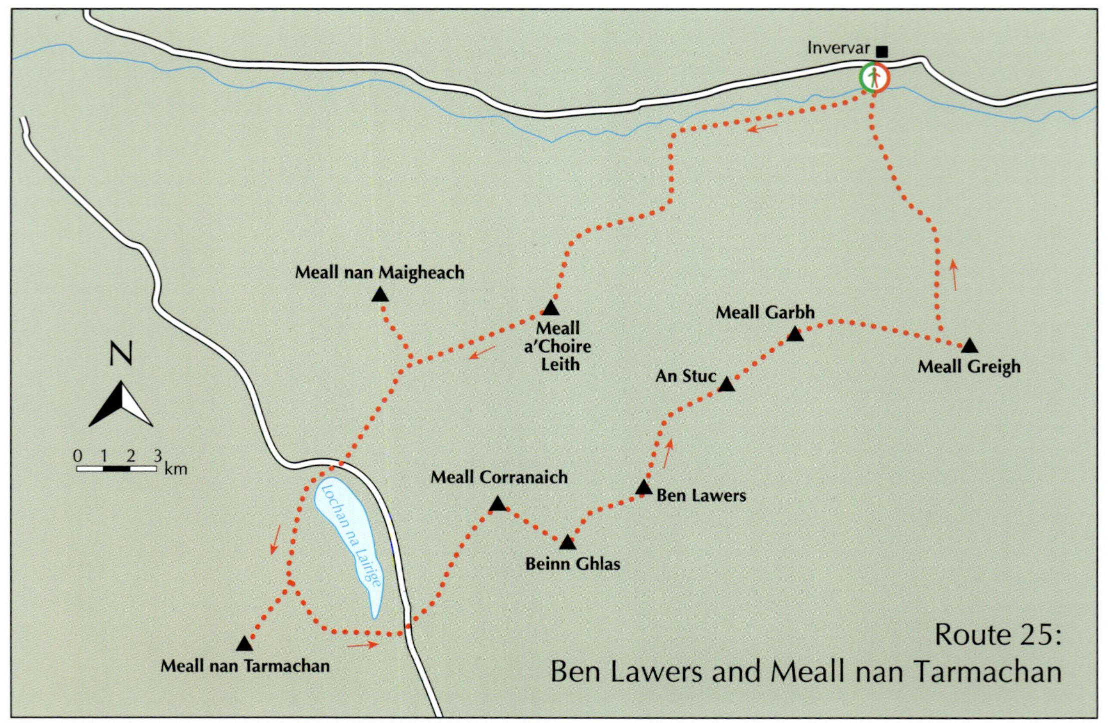
Invervar
Meall nan Maigheach
Meall Garbh
Meall a'Choire Leith
An Stuc
Meall Greigh
Meall Corranaich
Ben Lawers
Beinn Ghlas
Meall nan Tarmachan
Lochan na Lairige
N
0 1 2 3 km
Route 25:
Ben Lawers and Meall nan Tarmachan

the south side of this little hill you'll see the road reaching its high point at a cairn. Head towards this cairn and cross the road.

Now the rough slopes of **Meall nan Tarmachan**'s northern ridge presents itself. Climb south-west, keeping the crags of Creag an Lochain well to your left as you go. ▶

Once above Creag an Lochain there is a minor top to cross at 842m, and then the ridge dips slightly to the south.

Here there is a col with the tiny Lochan an Tairbh-uisge hidden in a hollow to the south. This makes a fine overnight campsite, and you could consider pitching up your tent first, then leaving your heavy gear behind while you climb Meall nan Tarmachan unencumbered.

The large expanse of **Lochan na Lairige** fills the bowl below.

Camping wild on the slopes of Meall nan Tarmachan

Above the lochan, at the col, there is a knoll and the ridge changes direction for a while. Follow the ridge westwards from the col with the knoll, for 150m, until you are established on the true north ridge of Meall nan Tarmachan. Turn southwards and ascend steadily to the

The superb east face of Meall nan Tarmachan

superb summit with its far reaching views. The top is marked by a cairn at 1043m (GR: NN585390).

If you've pitched camp at Lochan an Tairbh-uisge return the same way. If not, you can descend south-eastwards towards another subsidiary top and find some flat ground on which to camp there.

DAY 2

Wherever you spent the night, you need to start the day by making for the dam and the road at the south end of Lochan na Lairige. Go straight over the road and climb eastwards onto the **Sron Dha Mhurchaidh**. This is the south ridge of **Meall Corranaich**, the first Munro of the day. Turn northwards and climb the ridge veering to the north-east above Coire Odhar to gain the summit cairn at 1069m (GR: NN616410).

A steep but short descent to the south-east leads to a col, then a climb up the other side takes you to the fine summit of **Beinn Ghlas** at 1103m (GR: NN626404). There is no cairn on the highest point, but the huge drops on the north side leave you in no doubt as to where the highest point is. You are now established on the Ben Lawers ridge and well set for a grand traverse of these superb peaks.

Beinn Ghlas from Meall nan Tarmachan

Turn to the north-east and follow a well-trodden path along the ridge. Follow the path over a short rocky section, and then up to the summit of **Ben Lawers** at 1214m (GR: NN636414).

A much bigger cairn on the summit of Ben Lawers was built in 1878 in an effort to raise the mountain into the lofty company of Scotland's 4000' peaks, as the mountain itself only just fell short. Unfortunately the ruse failed as the cairn was viewed as a man-made structure, not part of the mountain, and in any case it collapsed soon afterwards.

The ridge going northwards from Ben Lawers is superbly exciting, but never too hard for a backpacker carrying a heavy load. The ridge drops immediately from the summit to a little bump at **Creag an Fhithich**, and then descends further to another col before the impressive cone of **An Stuc**.

The ascent up the south side of An Stuc is straightforward enough, but the descent to the col on the north side is very rocky and has been known to cause some people problems, especially in winter conditions. It really is not that hard, but if you are worried you can avoid the whole of An Stuc by going around its west and north sides at a much lower level. Once on the col to the north of An Stuc, the way up to **Meall Garbh** is easy. ◄

The summit is wonderfully airy, with its cairn being perched on a narrow crest at 918m (GR: NN644436).

Continue down the north-east ridge for 800m, then curve around to the east down broad flanks to a col. An easy ridge now leads for 2km east then south-east to the final Munro of the group, **Meall Greigh** at 1001m (GR: NN674438).

Return north-westwards along the ridge for 700m, then descend northwards over a very broad shoulder, curbing slightly to the north-east, then north, then north-west as you keep to the high ground. The ridge eventually drops you down towards a wide col before **Creag Dhubh**, and just before you reach this col you should veer off to the right (GR: NN665467). Aim for a path that runs down the east side of a burn in tight zigzags (GR: NN667469). Follow the path down along the outside of a small wood in the burn, reaching a track at Dericambus. Turn left along this track and follow it to the bridge over the river at **Invervar**.

ROUTE 26
The Trossachs from Balquhidder

Total Distance	38km
Daily Distances	Day 1 – 22km, Day 2 – 16km
Maps	Harvey Superwalker (Ben Ledi), OS Landranger sheet 57 (Stirling and the Trossachs)
Starting Point	Park sensibly in Balquhidder village, somewhere near the telephone box (GR: NN534208).

Area Summary

The hills of the Trossachs covered by this route are relatively unknown, despite being part of Loch Lomond and The Trossachs National Park. There are some very wild corners to be found here, once away from the glens. The hills taken by this route have Loch Voil and the Braes of Balquhidder to the north, and Strathyre to the east. Southwards, Strath Gartney forms a barrier, with its string of big lakes – Loch Venachar, Loch Achray, and Loch Katrine.

Route Summary

The route takes you south from Balquhidder, first into Glen Buckie and then onto a long ridge connecting the two Corbetts of Benvane and Ben Ledi. It then descends to the west to the shores of Glen Finglas Reservoir before heading north-west up Glen Finglas itself. The wild hills north of the glen and south of Loch Voil are then traversed before a final descent to Balquhidder.

Tourist Information

The nearest TIC is Callander (tel 01877 330342) and there is another in Killin (tel 01567 820254).

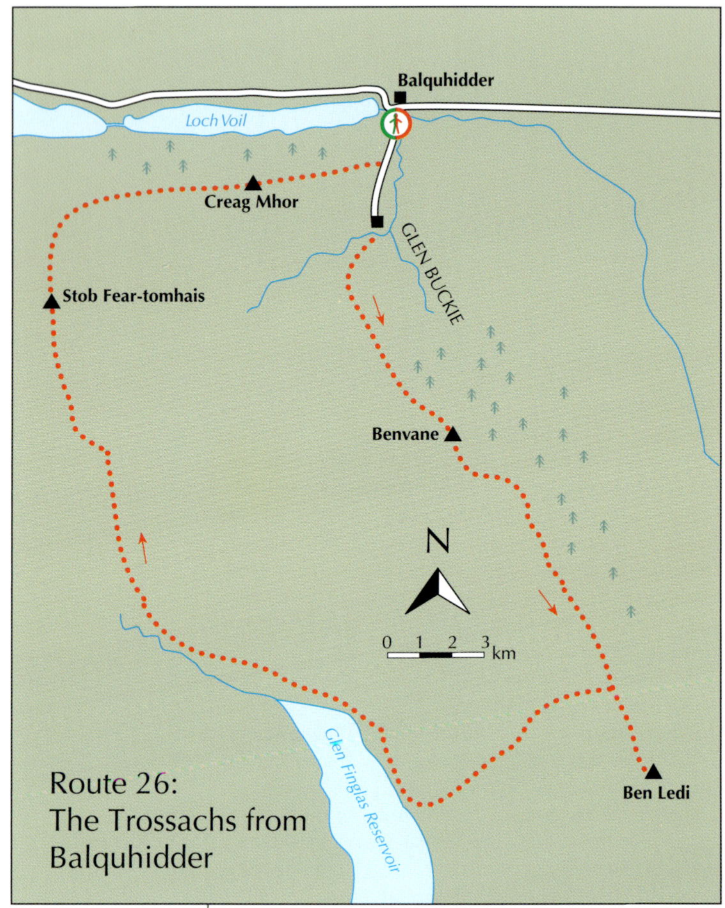

DAY 1

To the immediate west of **Balquhidder** Loch Voil stretches away into the distance to the head of Glengyle. At the eastern end of the loch, just south of the telephone box in the village, a bridge crosses over the River Balvag as it flows out of **Loch Voil**. Walk south over the bridge

Accommodation and Supplies
There are plenty of shops in Callander, as well as the usual B&B and hotel options. Call the TIC for ideas. The SYHA Hostel in Killin is another good place to stay (tel 01567 820546, website www.syha.org.uk).

Overnight Options
Camp wild by the banks of Finglas Water.

Escape Routes
Drop down to the west from Benvane or Ben Ledi to pick up the track north or south. From all other points on the route make for Glen Buckie and the road back to Balquhidder.

and bear left on the road at the first junction. Carry on to a crossroads in 300m, and here go straight ahead, continuing along the lane up **Glen Buckie**. Dead ahead you can see your first objective, the long north ridge of **Benvane** leading up to the summit. To your right is Creag Mhor, the hill that you will descend at the end of the day tomorrow.

This area is, of course, well known as Rob Roy country. Rob Roy MacGregor was born at Glengyle in 1671, and became one of Scotland's most notorious outlaws. However, his refusal to bow to the power of authority strikes a chord with many people, and he is, even today, thought of as being a clan hero. The MacGregor clan saw many bitter feuds with the clans from neighbouring glens, usually over land rights or cattle rustling, as well as an ongoing battle with the powerful Duke of Montrose. The feud with the Duke lead to Rob being outlawed and eventually captured and sentenced to transportation. He was however pardoned, and he returned to live a more peaceful life at Balquhidder where he stayed until his death in 1734. He is now buried in the churchyard in the village.

Ben Ledi's summit

Once you reach **Ballimore** at the end of the road turn left over a bridge that crosses the Calair Burn. Immediately you will see a path going westwards alongside the burn, and you should take this for 600m until you reach a little side stream.

Now turn southwards and follow the stream uphill, climbing steeply to gain the north ridge of Benvane at Lianach (GR: NN526158). The way to the summit of Benvane is obvious now, and all you have to do is keep to the ridge to the south-east. The summit is 2km along this ridge, and its top is marked by a cairn at 821m (GR: NN535137).

Turn to the south and descend to a couple of knolls on the ridge after 600m. Now the main ridge turns sharply to the north-east. Follow this gently downhill and continue to a flat area where it turns south-east to **Stuc Dhubh**. Climb over Stuc Dhubh, then continue in a gentle climb over rough, peaty ground to Bioran na Circe, a hill with a little lochan on its highest point, un-named on the Landranger map. The route now takes you southwards, down to a col where **Lochan nan Corp** nestles, then up the narrowing ridge to the summit of **Ben Ledi** at 879m (GR: NN563097).

Walk back northwards from the summit of Ben Ledi, as far as Bealach nan Corp, the small col just before Lochan nan Corp. Now descend steep slopes to the west, aiming for the track in Gleann Casaig. Once on the track high above burn, turn southwards and follow it downhill to sheepfold by a junction of tracks just above **Glen Finglas Reservoir** (GR: NN532090). Turn right here, down to the bridge over the Allt Ghleann Casaig. Cross over and follow the track to where the valley is split by the huge bulk of Meall Cala dead ahead. The two side glens each have tracks going up them, and at the foot of Meall Cala turn left, over the Allt Gleann nam Meann, and into the head of Glen Finglas. The route passes through some scattered deciduous woodland, and passes a sheepfold down on the left. This is a good area to be thinking about camping for the night.

DAY 2

Follow the track westwards, until you are climbing the steep slopes at the head of the valley. Continue to where the track takes a big swing to the north, and here leave it to head westwards up the hill to gain the ridge of Sron a'Chaorainn. Now turn northwards along the ridge, climbing easily along **Cnoc Odhar** to the summit of **Creagan nan Sgiath** at 697m (GR: NN484143).

Drop down westwards to a col, then climb up to the west to gain the ridge of **Beinn Bhreac**. This is the southern arm of **Stob Fear-tomhais**. Turn northwards along the ridge and climb beyond a col to the summit of this fine little Corbett at 771m (GR: NN474163).

The name Stob Fear-tomhais does not appear on any of the OS maps. The summit has an OS trig pillar, and the locals down in the glen to the north simply know the mountain as the surveyor's peak. Stob Fear-tomhais is the Gaelic for this. The mountain used to be called Ceann na Baintighearna, but that name refers to the northern subsidiary top at 701m.

Head northwards from the summit of Stob Fear-tomhais, dropping down its north ridge to a col. Continue northwards, veering off to visit Ceann na Baintighearna if you wish (GR: NN471177). The way down follows the long north-east ridge from a shoulder just east of the summit of Ceann na Baintighearna, and this leads down towards the dark forests that cloak the southern side of Loch Voil. Do not descend all the way to the forest line, but turn to the east to reach **Bealach Driseach** (GR: NN493183). From the bealach climb eastwards to the western top of **Creag Mhor**, then continue eastwards to the actual summit of this Graham at 657m (GR: NN511185).

Now descend hummocky ground eastwards, curving around to the north-east along the ridge that takes you down to the edge of the forest below. Follow the forest edge eastwards to pick up the lane between Balquhidder and Glen Buckie. Turn left along this lane to return to Balquhidder.

ROUTE 27
The Munros of Glen Creran

Total Distance	42km
Daily Distances	Day 1 – 20km, Day 2 – 22km
Maps	Harvey British Mountain Map 1:40,000 (Ben Nevis & Glen Coe)
Starting Point	Car park at the head of Glen Creran (GR: NN036488)

Area Summary

There are three Munros ranged around Loch Creran, and while they are occasionally climbed from Glen Coe or Glen Etive, a round of all three in one expedition from Loch Creran is superb. Glen Creran itself rises at the head of these mountains, backing on to the great peaks of Glen Coe, and Loch Creran runs out into the southern end of Loch Linnhe where the two merge to become the Firth of Lorn.

Route Summary

This is a tough route, taking in the three Munros of the area. The route starts by heading south to the foot of Beinn Sgulaird. This is then traversed before a high campsite is found beneath Beinn Fhionnlaidh. On the second day Beinn Fhionnlaidh is followed by a traverse of Sgor na h-Ulaidh before tracks are picked up back into the head of Glen Creran.

DAY 1

From the car park at the head of Glen Creran take the lane eastwards, passing the few houses at **Elleric**. The lane becomes a track behind the farm at Glenure, and you should bear right, down to the river where you'll find a bridge. Cross to the south side of the River Ure and turn westwards, following a track above forest plantations. Continue to the east side of **Loch Baile Mhic Chailein**,

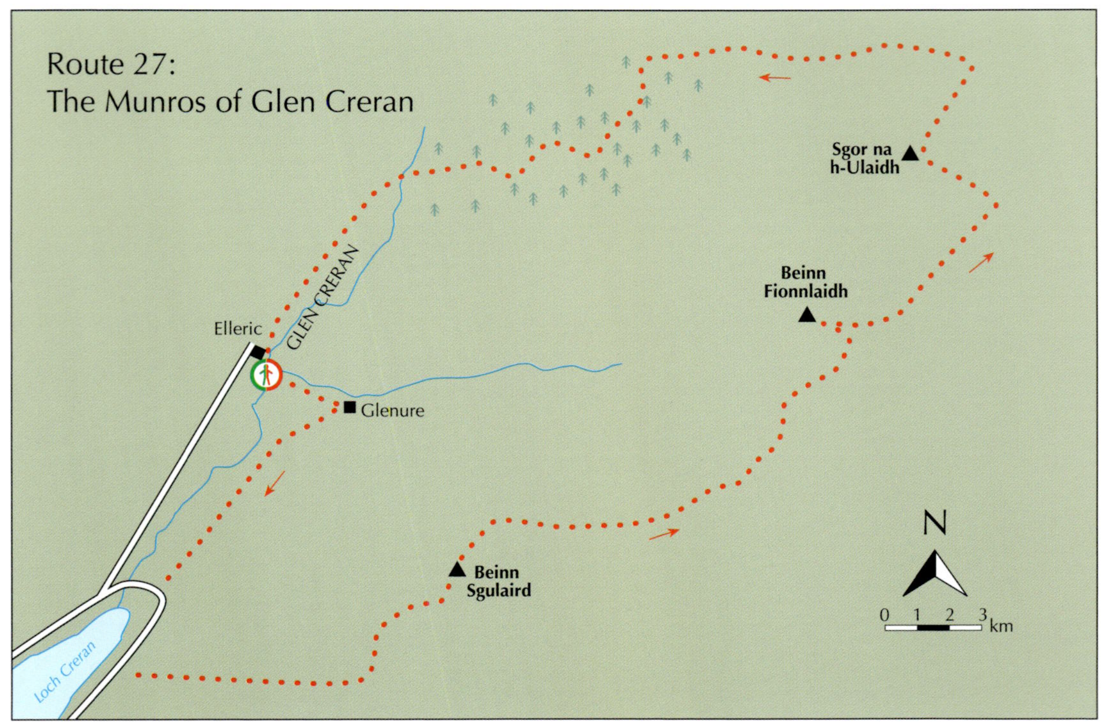
Route 27:
The Munros of Glen Creran
GLEN CRERAN
Elleric
Glenure
Sgor na h-Ulaidh
Beinn Fionnlaidh
Beinn Sgulaird
Loch Creran
N
0 1 2 3 km

Tourist Information
There's a TIC in Oban (tel 01631 563122).

Accommodation and Supplies
There's a campsite at Barcaldine, on the south side of Loch Creran (tel 01631 720348), and lots of B&B options in Oban.

Overnight Options
Camp wild along the route.

Escape Routes
Drop down any of the westwards-facing corries into Glen Creran.

then walk on to the south-west to the farm at Taraphocain. The track continues to the south-west and brings you out on the road that runs around the head of **Loch Creran**. Turn left along the road for 700m. There's a belt of coniferous trees here, and where this ends on the left, you'll see a path cutting up through the trees to the south-east. Follow this, climbing steeply uphill above the Allt Buidhe. The path keeps to the north side of the Allt Buidhe throughout, and you should follow it right up to the col at the head of the corrie (GR: NN044441).

To the north of the col there is a 300m ascent to the south-western peak of the **Beinn Sgulaird** range. The going is steep and rocky in places, but if you keep just to the right of the crest it is never too difficult. You'll soon find yourself on the south-west peak at 863m (GR: NN043447). Turn to the north-east and drop onto a dip before the middle peak. Climb up and over this, then down into another col before the lovely curving arête of Beinn Sgulaird's summit ridge is gained. Follow this ridge north-eastwards, curving around to the north to reach the top at 937m (GR: NN053461).

To the north-east of the summit is a little shoulder, and at this point the ridge splits. Go down to the shoulder, 250m from the summit, to where you'll find a little

Beinn Sgulaird's summit slopes in winter

knoll at 909m. Head north along the steep ridge, descending in a big arc to the north-east, then eastwards down to a col with a tiny lochan nestling in it (GR: NN063466). Immediately east of the lochan is the rocky wart of **Stob Gaibhre**. Climb over this then continue along the east ridge to a spot height at 416m (GR: NN075468).

Just below this spot height to its north-east there are a couple of lochans, and at the lower end of the most westerly of these, **Airidh nan Lochan**, where the stream gushes out, there is a footbridge. Head downhill in this direction and you'll reach another side stream before you get to this bridge. There is another footbridge over the first side stream just to the left. Cross both bridges and walk up to Airidh nan Lochan. Now walk eastwards to the second lochan and follow a compass bearing north-eastwards around the eastern flanks of **An Grianan**, aiming for **Lochan na Fola**. This makes a superb place to camp for the night.

DAY 2

Climb up to the north, across a vague ridge until you are beneath a broken ridge to the east with a tiny lochan high up on its flanks (GR: NN094488). Climb the gully to the left of the ridge until you are on the shoulder just above the lochan, then head just east of north to the col high up on the east ridge of **Beinn Fhionnlaidh** at 795m (GR: NN103498). The way up is steep, but the ridge is soon gained. Turn westwards along the ridge and follow it to the summit of Beinn Fhionnlaidh at 959m (GR: NN095497).

Return along the east ridge of the mountain, dropping to the col at 795m. To the north-east is the col that connects Beinn Fhionnlaidh to the next Munro, **Sgor na h-Ulaidh**. There are two ways of reaching this col, both of them steep and rocky. From point 795m you can descend first to the north-west, the cut back to the north-east and so down to the col. The other option is to climb eastwards from 795m to the eastern peak at 841m (GR: NN107498). From there you can descend the rocky north-east ridge. There are a few short steps that need to be scrambled down, but the col below is soon reached.

From the col at 451m (GR: NN111505) climb north-eastwards up to a broad col on Sgor na h-Ulaidh's south-east ridge (GR: NN117513). Turn to the north-west from the col and follow the rocky ridge to the summit at 994m (GR: NN112517).

Descend to the north-east along a ridge to a col, then climb up the other side to **Stob an Fhuarain** at 968m. Head northwards from there for 300m, then descend the slopes to the north-west until it is possible to cut back to the south-west across the head of the corrie. You are aiming for the col (GR: NN103524) that lies between Sgor na h-Ulaidh and Meall Lighiche.

From the col descend diagonally to the right, keeping above the stream. When you reach the edge of the forest keep above it, heading westwards until you are above the deep V-shaped cleft below Meall an Aodainn (GR: NN084522). Now descend into the forest southwards. The going is hard as there is no path and the trees

*Beinn Fhionnlaidh
from Loch Creran*

are close together. However, if you keep close to the stream you will hit a path within 300m, and this cuts diagonally down the hillside. Follow this path to the west, continuing where it becomes a track. Cross the Allt Eilidh and walk on to the farm at Salachail (GR: NN056511). The track now runs south-westwards, keeping above the **River Creran**, and so back to the car park at the road-end.

ROUTE 28

Ben Lomond and the shores of Loch Lomond

Total Distance	42km
Daily Distances	Day 1 – 26km, Day 2 – 16km
Maps	Harvey Superwalker (Ben Lomond)
Starting Point	Car park at Rowardennan (GR: NS361985)

Area Summary

The shores of Loch Lomond barely need an introduction. Being just a short drive north of Glasgow, the loch itself, its wooded flanks, and the mountains that ring it are all very popular indeed. The eastern side of the loch gets its fair share of visitors, and it is here that you'll find Ben Lomond, the most southerly of all the Munros. To the north of Ben Lomond the hills are little visited however, and there you're guaranteed a little more solitude.

Route Summary

The route starts by taking the 'tourist path' up Ben Lomond from Rowardennan. From there you branch out, leaving the tourists behind as you cross many rough kilometres to reach Beinn a'Chroin, a remote Corbett to the north of Loch Arklet. You then follow a steep and rough route down to pick up the West Highland Way, which you follow to the south back to Rowardennan.

Tourist Information

There's a TIC at Balloch (tel 01389 753533).

Accommodation and Supplies

There are various campsites scattered along the shores of Loch Lomond – try the Forestry Commission site at Cashel (tel 01360 870234), or the site at Milarrochy Bay (tel 01360 870236), while the SYHA Hostel at

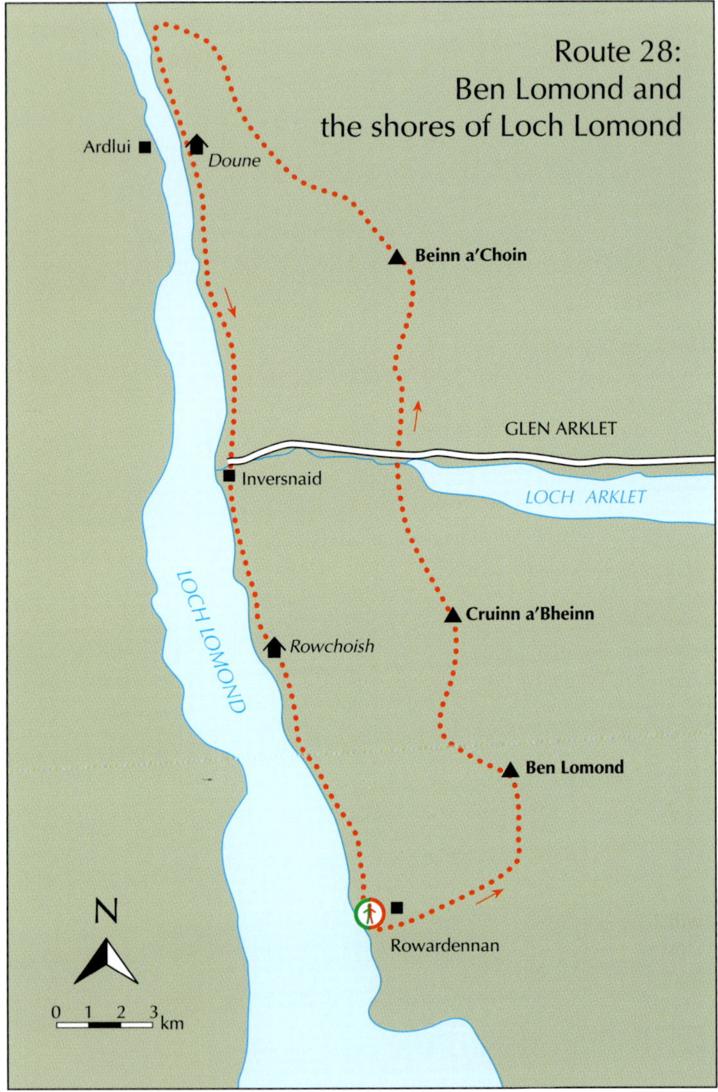

Route 28:
Ben Lomond and
the shores of Loch Lomond
Ardlui
Doune
Beinn a'Choin
GLEN ARKLET
Inversnaid
LOCH ARKLET
LOCH LOMOND
Cruinn a'Bheinn
Rowchoish
Ben Lomond
Rowardennan
N
0 1 2 3 km

Rowardennan (tel 01360 870273, website www.syha.org.uk) is right at the start of the route.

Overnight Options
Camp wild along the route or use the bothy at Doune near the northern end of Loch Lomond (GR: NN332144).

Escape Routes
Aim for the shores of Loch Lomond and follow the West Highland Way in either direction.

DAY 1

At the southern end of the car parking area at **Rowardennan** there is a small picnic site next to a burn. The path up **Ben Lomond** starts here. Follow it north-eastwards through a break in the forest, crossing a footbridge at Creagan Breac, then emerging from the forest at a second footbridge in Coire Corrach. Here the path takes to the open hillside, taking you north-eastwards up onto the open ridge of **Sron Aonaich** where it turns northwards. The going is easy and the route is not at all hard to follow. Above Sron Aonaich the ridge gets a little narrower, with Coire Odhar falling away to the west and the knolly ground around Sithean lying to the right. Continue upwards to where the ridge narrows properly now, and follow it north-westwards to the fine summit ridge. Handrail along this, going westwards and round to the summit cairn and trig pillar at 974m (GR: NN367028).

All of the tourists that you've shared the climb with will be returning via the same route as the ascent. However, you should take the rocky north-west ridge from the summit, dropping steeply towards a flatter area. Beyond this flat point the ridge turns northwards and is much more gently angled. Follow it northwards down to a col, with the dome of **Cruinn a'Bheinn** standing dead ahead throughout.

Ben Lomond from across Loch Lomond

From the col the ascent of Cruinn a'Bheinn is straightforward, and if you sit on the summit at 633m (GR: NN366052) and look back towards Ben Lomond you get a rare view into the superb northern corries of the Munro.

Head north-westwards down easy slopes, aiming for the high point of a track that cuts across the hill from Cailness to Gleann Gaoithe. At the high point (GR: NN354066) take a bearing just west of north to the lovely little tarn at **Lochan Cruachan**, then climb to the top of the compact peak of **Cruachan** at 537m, that overlooks it, just to the north.

Head north down the broad moorland flanks of Cruachan, aiming for the dam at the foot of **Loch Arklet** (GR: NN355093). Below the dam there is a bridge that leads over the river and out onto the minor road running through Glen Arklet.

Go straight over the road and climb diagonally to the north across the broken slopes of **Stob an Fhainne**.

Your objective is the col to the north of Stob an Fhainne, known as Bealach a'Mheim (GR: NN358121), and to get there the best route is to skirt along below the craggy ground on the west side of Stob an Fhainne, or alternatively, to go over the top then down into the col.

Once on Bealach a'Mheim walk northwards up the final slopes of **Beinn a'Chroin**, climbing a vague ridge until you are just a short way east of the summit. Turn left and head up to the top of this fine little Corbett at 770m (GR: NN354130).

The best place for you to spend the night is at the bothy at **Doune** (GR: NN332144), but to get there involves crossing some steep and craggy ground. The best route from Beinn a'Chroin is to go northwards from the summit along a ridge, then curve to the north-west on the continuation of this and down to Lochan Dubh (GR: NN344141). Walk northwards over the small hill of **Stob nan Eighrach** at 613m, then just west of north down to Lochan nam Muc (GR: NN341152). Now walk to the north-west for 800m, and you'll will find the hillside to the west now falling more gently down to the northern tip of **Loch Lomond**. Descend to the track near Ardleish (GR: NN327155).

This track is the West Highland Way, a well-blazed trail, and if you turn southwards along this for 1.6km you will reach the welcoming bothy at Doune (GR: NN332144).

DAY 2

Today's route needs little in the way of description, as it follows the West Highland Way southwards all the way back to Rowardennan. Having said that, nearly all the people (of which there are many) doing the West Highland Way do so in a south to north direction, so you will be heading the 'wrong' way. ▶ Head first for Pollochro, then through the Inversnaid Nature Reserve to reach the Inversnaid Hotel (GR: NN337089).

Continue southwards to the little cottage at Cailness, cross the river and continue for 1.5km to a junction. Go right here, down to a point just above the bothy at

The walking here along the shores of Loch Lomond is lovely, passing through lots of deciduous woodland.

Ben Lomond from across Loch Lomond

Rowchoish (GR: NN336044), then carry on along the West Highland Way, keeping to the shore-side path throughout.

You soon find yourself at Ptarmigan Lodge, and from there it is a short stroll back to Rowardennan.

ROUTE 29
The East Coast of Islay

Total Distance	43km
Daily Distances	Day 1 – 23km, Day 2 – 21km
Maps	OS Landranger sheet 60 (Islay)
Starting Point	The ferry terminal at Port Askaig, on the north-east side of Islay (GR: NR432693)
Finishing Point	The ferry terminal at Port Ellen, on the south side of Islay (GR: NR364451)

Area Summary

Islay (pronounced 'eye-la') is the most southern of the Hebridean islands. It is by no means the roughest, wildest or mountainous, although it does have some superbly wild coastlines, and remote hills, and it does have one redeeming feature that makes it worth a visit even if you don't want to go walking – single malt whisky. This small island with a population of around 4000 has no less than eight distilleries.

The island has some fabulous rocky coastlines, as well as incredible beaches. The interior is a mixture of rough moorland and rough farmland. The east coast, overlooking the Sound of Islay, is by far the wildest part of the island.

Route Summary

This route links the two ferry terminals, Port Askaig and Port Ellen. Initially the route follows the coast itself, as far as the superbly situated McArthur's Head. It then takes you inland to the island's highest peaks, Glas Bheinn, and Beinn Bheigier before leading you southwards to Port Ellen. Although never mountainous, this is a remote route through wild and rough country, and it shouldn't be underestimated.

Tourist Information
There's a TIC at Bowmore (tel 01496 810254). To get to Islay you need to get to Kennacraig from Glasgow. There's a bus service (tel 0141 3327133) from Buchanan Street bus station which connects with the ferry from Kennacraig. Ferries from Kennacraig go to both Port Askaig, and to Port Ellen. They are operated by Caledonian MacBrayne (tel 01880 730253, Kennacraig Office, and tel 01496 302209, Port Ellen Office). For getting around Islay there is a regular bus service with Islay Coaches (tel 01496 840273).

Accommodation and Supplies
There are plenty of places to stay in Port Askaig, Port Ellen, and in the island's capital, Bowmore. Call the TIC in Bowmore for ideas.

Overnight Options
Camp wild along the route.

Escape Routes
Until you reach McArthur's Head, the only feasible route of escape is to go back the way you've come. Once you reach the headland however, there is a path that leads south along the shore to the road head at Claggain Bay.

The views across the Sound of Islay to Jura are incredible, the scene being dominated by the bulky domes of the Paps of Jura.

DAY 1
From the ferry terminal at **Port Askaig** you should begin by heading along the shore beneath the woodlands of Dunlossit House. Once past the woods you'll reach a little lighthouse down on the shore, and from there onwards you can walk above the shore. Continue southwards to the small bay at **Fionn-phort**, then climb up and over the rocky headland at Am Meall. Here you enter rough woodland again, and you immediately feel as though you are very cut off from the outside world. ◀

As you push on further south, covering a lot of rough, pathless ground, you begin to climb upwards slightly around the eastern flanks of **Beinn Dubh**. The route then takes you down into Glen Logan where you need to cross the small stream before heading on below the crags of **An Cladach**. Around the ridge you'll reach the wild corrie of Gleann Ghaireasdail with the

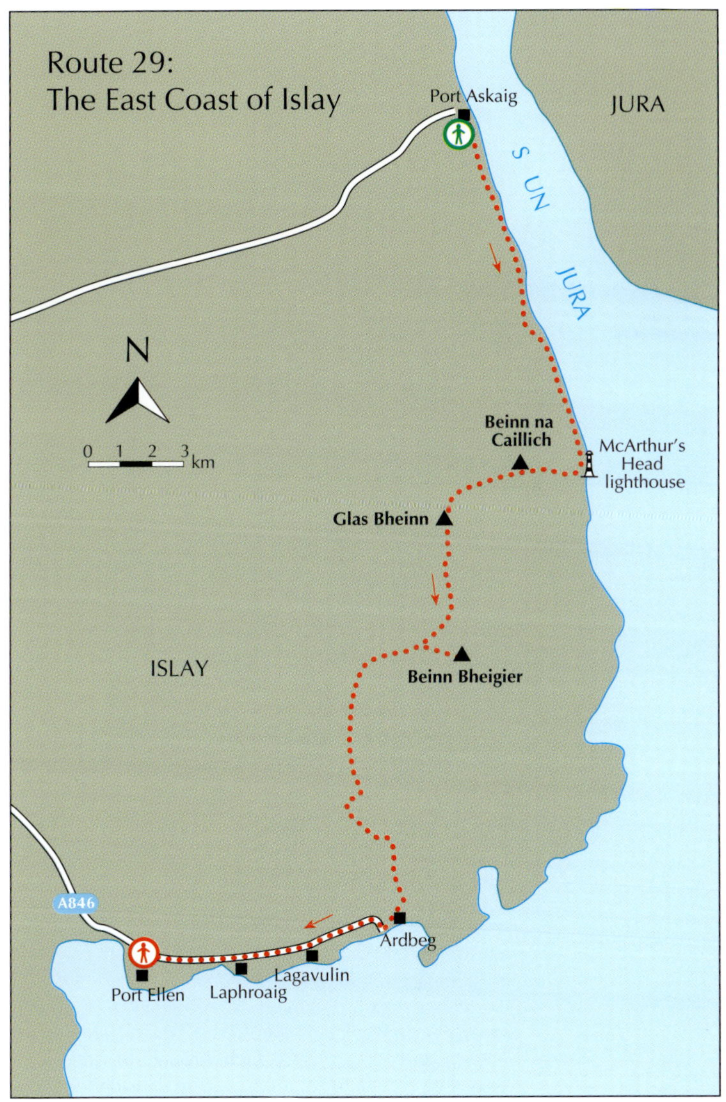
Route 29:
The East Coast of Islay
Port Askaig
JURA
SUND OF JURA
N
0 1 2 3 km
Beinn na Caillich
McArthur's Head lighthouse
Glas Bheinn
ISLAY
Beinn Bheigier
A846
Port Ellen
Laphroaig
Lagavulin
Ardbeg

Port Askaig on Islay

spectacular peak of **Sgorr nam Faoileann** rising above. You can climb up here if you wish, and so follow a ridge on to Glas Bheinn, but that would mean missing out on McArthur's Head which would be a real pity.

Continue around the rough slopes to Gleann Choireadail.

What a fantastic name Gleann Choireadail is! It is part Gaelic and part Old Norse, and is basically three different words all meaning 'valley' (glen, corrie, and dale). It translates roughly as 'the valley of the hanging valley, of the valley'!

Now climb up to about 100m above the sea to continue the traverse to McArthur's Head. There are some big cliffs just below you here, and to pass them you need to gain this extra height.

As you come around to McArthur's Head you can drop down to the lighthouse that stands on the headland.

Southwards now there is a path, and if the weather is poor you could take this around the coast all the way through to Ardbeag. However, if all is going well and you want to tackle some of the peaks of the island you can start by ascending **Beinn na Caillich**, immediately above McArthur's Head. Climb south-westwards at first, to the flat shoulder of Beinn na Caillich Beag, then turn to the north-west to gain the main top's summit at 332m (GR: NR450596).

Now follow the ridge westwards, down into a col then continuing along a switchback to a rocky bluff below the east ridge of **Glas Bheinn**. Climb southwards to gain this east ridge, then turn to the west and follow it over little rock steps to the summit at 472m (GR: NR429592).

The views now are superb, taking in the Paps of Jura to the north-east, and the whole of Islay to the west. This is a good place to look for golden eagles, as a pair have these hills as their breeding territory.

Head south from Glas Bheinn for 1km, then turn south-westwards with the ridge as it curves around the compact western corrie of the mountain. From this arm-like ridge drop down to the south, to a col between Glas Bheinn and **Am Mam**. Continue southwards to the top of Am Mam (GR: NR426575).

South again from Am Mam is a lower col, and once you've descended to this you might want to think about where to camp for the night. The head of the corrie to the west, Poll Gorm is a good spot, as is the small tarn, Loch a'Mhuillin-ghaoithe up on the ridge of Lorg Reidh to the south-west.

DAY 2

Wherever you camped last night, start the day by making for the ridge of Lorg Reidh, just up and to the north-east of Loch a'Mhuillin-ghaoithe. To the south-east of this ridge lies the highest mountain on Islay, **Beinn Bheigier**, which should not be missed. Climb up the scree-covered slopes of the north-west ridge, which brings you out at the summit trig pillar at 491m (GR: NR430564).

Islay's wild east coast

Return down the same route to Lorg Reidh, perhaps to pick up your heavy backpacking gear before heading off.

To the south-west of Loch a'Mhuillin-ghaoithe there is a broad ridge and you should follow this, curving southwards with **Loch nam Bhreac** to your right as you go. Go over a minor peak, then continue on a narrowing ridge to the south-west to **Beinn Uraraidh**'s top at 456m (GR: NR406542). There is a cairn on the highest point.

Southwards from Beinn Uraraidh lies **Loch Beinn Uraraidh**, and you should cross the rough ground below you to reach the loch's eastern side. Go south again, heading around another small lochan, then continuing southwards downhill to a col just before you reach **Loch Leathann an Sgorra** to the west, and Loch Dearg an Sgorra to the east. Pass between the two lochs and climb up to the south for 500m before turning south-west to visit the summit of **Sgorr Bhogachain** at 374m (GR: NR400515).

Head south-westwards across the small flat area of moorland below the summit cone, then descend south-wards again to Loch Uigeadail (GR: NR405506).

Walk clockwise around the loch to its outfall, where you'll pick up a path that runs southwards down the hill, keeping the burn to the east for a while.

Lower down the hill, at a col before the knoll of **Cnoc Crun na Maoil** the stream veers away to the east, but the path continues southwards, passing to the west of Cnoc Crun na Maoil. Continue to the old shelter at Solam, then descend on the path through the woodlands of Airigh nam Beist, going over a burn and turning left to a good track coming down from Loch Iarnan. Turn right along the track and follow it down to the road at **Ardbeg**, just above the distillery.

It's a pleasant walk along the road westwards to **Port Ellen**, taking you past Lagavulin and Laphroaig distilleries before you reach the outskirts of the small town. The ferry terminal lies at the western end of the harbour.

ROUTE 30
Arran's High Hills

Total Distance	43km
Daily Distances	Day 1 – 25km, Day 2 – 18km
Maps	Harvey Superwalker (Arran)
Starting Point	The ferry terminal at Brodick (GR: NS022360).

Area Summary

Arran is an island of two halves. The northern end is very rocky and mountainous, being composed chiefly of granite, which makes some of the peaks very hard to climb even for rock climbers. The southern half of the island is more genteel, and that is where most of the tourists can be found. The island is the furthest south of any of the main Scottish islands, and some might say that it does not belong in a book about the Southern Highlands. That is a fair claim, but it definitely belongs to the Highlands in character, rather than the lowlands, and so I make no apologies for its inclusion.

Route Summary

This route takes you right into the heart of the mountains, and gives you the opportunity to scale the four Corbetts of the island. The route is superbly varied, and follows paths and tracks for most of the way. Once you've crossed the range at the head of Glen Rosa, the route takes you down to the wild north-east coast, which is followed to Lochranza on the northern tip of the island. The return leg takes a different route through the mountains and involves some wonderful easy scrambling along the spine of a spectacular granite ridge.

Tourist Information
There's a TIC at Brodick next to the ferry terminal pier (tel 01770 302140). Caledonian MacBrayne operates the ferries to the island (tel Ardrossan office 01294 463470, or Brodick office 01770 302166).

Accommodation and Supplies
Ideally you should camp at Glen Rosa, just a short walk from the pier terminal at Brodick. The site is a basic one, but is right at the start of your route into the hills (tel 01770 302380, website www.glenrosa.com). Brodick has shops and other accommodation in the form of the usual B&Bs and hotels. Call the TIC for details.

Overnight Options
Camp at Lochranza Golf and Camping Park (tel 01770 830273, website www.lochnranzegolf.com), or use the SYHA Hostel (tel 01770 830631, website www.syha.org.uk) there.

Escape Routes
From the southern side of the mountains, descend Glen Rosa to Brodick, and from the northern side descend Gleann Easan Biorach to Lochranza.

DAY 1
From the **Glen Rosa campsite** (GR: NS002376) head up the west side of the glen, following the track throughout and crossing the Garbh Allt at a footbridge (GR: NR983386). ▶ After 3km the path splits at a junction by a stream. Take the path to the right, crossing the stream and climbing steeply northwards towards the distant col known as **The Saddle**.

From the col you can make ascents of either of the peaks to the side. **Goatfell** (GR: NR992415) lies to the south-east and at 874m is the highest mountain on the island. **Cir Mhor** (GR: NR973431) lies to the west and has a rough path going up and over slabs to its summit at 799m.

Descend the north-east side of the Saddle into the head of lovely **Glen Sannox**. The path initially takes you

The way continues northwards towards the fantastic ring of high and rocky peaks that circle the valley.

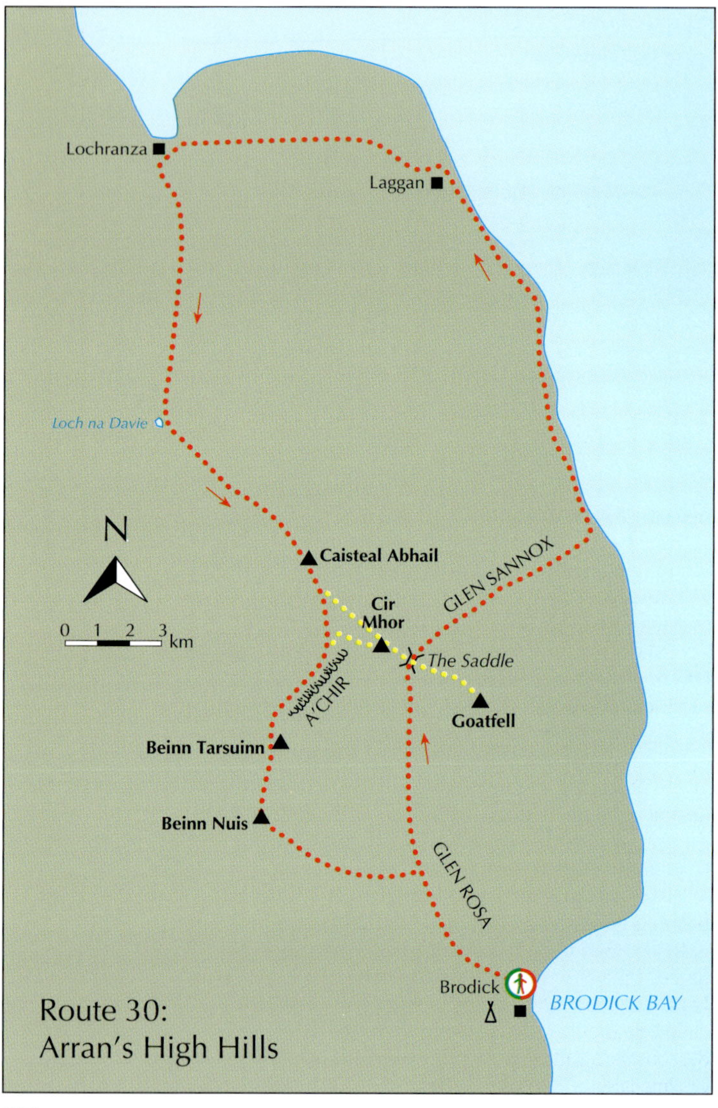

Route 30:
Arran's High Hills

down to the north-west side of the burn, but then lower down it crosses over at a footbridge. Descend now along the south side of the Sannox Burn to a track at South Sannox, and out onto the road (A841). Go left for a few metres, then down to some steeping stones on the right, that take you back over the Sannox Burn and onto the beach. Just above the shoreline there is a path that heads north along the coast. Follow this to where the North Sannox Burn enters the sea (GR: NS015465). Cross the river here and continue along the coastal path heading north. The route passes below the woodlands of Leac Gharbh, and out to the Fallen Rocks below the cliffs of Corloch. Stay on the path throughout, continuing beyond **Millstone Point** to **Laggan** where the path splits.

At the Laggan junction turn steeply uphill to the left, behind the building, and climb directly up for 300m until the track swings away to the west and cuts diagonally, and more easily, across the face of Creag Ghlas Laggan. It eventually reaches the top of the hill at a col called Bearradh Tom a'Muidhe, then begins the easy descent alongside the Allt Chailean down into Glen Chalmadale.

Goatfell is Arran's highest mountain

You gain a track here where you meet the first houses, and this bends around to the north-west. Just past the bend there is a path going off on the left down to the river. Follow this and cross over via the footbridge to the **Lochranza** campsite at the golf course. Alternatively, continue along the track down to the road junction, where you can turn left for the youth hostel.

DAY 2
Start the day by heading south-east along the A841 out of Lochranza. Where it bends to the left to cross the river there is a path that leaves the run on the right. Follow this up the west side of the burn and into **Gleann Easan Biorach**. The path stays on the west side of the burn throughout, right up to the wonderful setting of **Loch na Davie** (GR: NR950457) on the col at the head of the glen.

You can now leave the path and follow the ridge to the south-east, climbing up stony ground to reach Carn Mor at 685m (GR: NR960451). Here you'll pick up a path that runs south-eastwards along the narrow ridge towards **Caisteal Abhail**. Follow this ridge to the summit of the Corbett at 859m (GR: NR968443).

Leave the summit by descending south-westwards along the path, following this as it curves around to the south above Coire na h-Uaimh.

Ahead of you along the ridge is Cir Mhor, and you could climb this from here, if you didn't bag it yesterday from the Saddle. In that case, follow the path along the ridge, then where the path splits before the final slopes, take the left-hand path straight up the ridge to the summit. Return along the ridge westward, but take the left-hand path to follow the south-west ridge and regain the main route.

To by-pass Cir Mhor, continue along the path which veers off to the right instead of following the ridge path eastwards to the summit – the two paths meet again on the south-west ridge just below the summit (GR: NR967429).

Ahead now, going south-westwards, the ridge drops to 591m, then comes up abruptly to the foot of a difficult section of the ridge. Avoid this, the **A'Chir** traverse, by dropping down to the west slightly, following the path throughout. This takes you below the crest of the difficult section, over easy ground, and brings you back onto the ridge south of A' Chir at Bealach an **Fhir-bhogha** where there is a cairn (GR: NR963415).

Go south-westwards up the steep north-east ridge of **Beinn Tarsuinn** to the summit at 826m (GR: NR959413), then continue to the south to an intermediate top at 796m. ▶ Continue along the path, following it to **Beinn Nuis** at 792m (GR: NR955398). Here the ridge now turns to the south-east, and you should follow it down to where the slopes ease in gradient, taking you down to the Garbh Allt. Stay on the north side of the stream until you reach the footbridge that you crossed yesterday morning. Go over the bridge and follow the track back to the **Glen Rosa** campsite, having conquered the four Corbetts of Arran.

Superb granite peaks await the walker on Arran

Again the path leads along the superb ridge, with spectacular views down into the wild and rocky corries to the east.

APPENDIX 1
Useful Websites

The author runs regular navigation and other skills courses for hillwalkers and mountaineers www.wildridgeadventure.com.

Wilderness Scotland
www.wildernessscotland.com

The Scottish Tourist Board
www.visitscotland.com

The Mountain Bothy Association
www.mountainbothies.org.uk

The Backpacker's Club
www.backpackersclub.co.uk

Cicerone Press
www.cicerone.co.uk

Harvey Maps
www.harveymaps.co.uk

Mountain Weather Information Service
www.mwis.org.uk

APPENDIX 2
Bibliography

The most useful general mountain guidebooks for Scotland are the district guides published by the Scottish Mountaineering Trust.

A superb book for anyone interested in upland wildlife is *Hostile Habitats*, also published by the Scottish Mountaineering Trust.

For field guides and other books on wildlife I find that the Christopher Helm, Poyser and Pica Press books are invaluable. These are all imprints of A&C Black, and their website gives full details: www.acblack.com/christopherhelm.

For the islands of Scotland the only book worth considering is *The Scottish Islands* by Hamish Haswell Smith, published by Canongate: www.canongate.net.

For more practical advice, try the *Mountain Skills Training Handbook*, by Pete Hill and Stuart Johnson (published by David and Charles 2004).

APPENDIX 3

Route Summary Table

No	Route	Start/Finish	Distance	Days	Maps	Difficulty
1	The Monadhliath to Kingussie	Aviemore – Kingussie	36km	2	OS Landranger 35	Moderate
2	Through Glen Roy from Laggan	Melgarve –Roybridge	28km	2	OS Landranger 34	Easy
3	Glen Einich and the Great Moss	Whitewell, near Aviemore	44km	2	Harvey BMM Cairngorms & Lochnagar	Strenuous
4	Through the Lairig Ghru	Coylumbridge – Linn of Dee	30km	2	Harvey BMM Cairngorms & Lochnagar	Easy
5	The Lairig an Laoigh	Linn of Dee – Glenmore	32km	2	Harvey BMM Cairngorms & Lochnagar	Easy
6	The Eastern Cairngorms	Linn of Quoich	44km	2	Harvey BMM Cairngorms & Lochnagar	Strenuous
7	Cairngorms High Level Traverse	Linn of Dee	69km	4	Harvey BMM Cairngorms & Lochnagar	Challenging
8	Glen Muick High Level Circuit	Spittal of Glenmuick	32km	2	Harvey BMM Cairngorms & Lochnagar	Strenuous
9	Glen Lee and Glen Mark	Glen Esk	40km	2	OS Landranger 44	Moderate

10	Mount Battock and Clachnaben	Millden Lodge in Glen Esk	55km	2	OS Landranger 44 & 45	Easy
11	Jock's Road and Tolmount	Glen Doll	42km	2	OS Landranger 43 & 44	Moderate
12	The Glenshee Munros	Spittal of Glenshee	40km	2	Harvey BMM Cairngorms & Lochnagar	Strenuous
13	The Blair Atholl Munros	Blair Atholl	50km	2	OS Landranger 43	Strenuous
14	The Grampian Glens Traverse	Blair Atholl	86km	4	OS Landranger 43	Easy
15	The Scottish 4000'ers Traverse	Glenmore – Fort William	143km	7	OS Landranger 36. 43, 42 & 41; Harvey BMM Ben Nevis; Cairngorms	Challenging
16	The Ben Alder Forest	Corrour railway station	50km	2	OS Landranger 42 & 41	Challenging
17	The Glen Nevis Traverse	Glen Nevis Youth Hostel	57km	2	Harvey BMM Ben Nevis	Challenging
18	Fort William to Dalwhinnie	Fort William – Dalwhinnie	65km	3	OS Landranger 41 & 42	Easy
19	Glen Coe from Appin	Glen Creran	35km	2	Harvey BMM Ben Nevis	Moderate
20	Mull's Wilderness Coast	Loch Scridain	28km	2	OS Explorer 375	Strenuous
21	The Black Mount	Victoria Bridge	48km	3	OS Landranger 50	Challenging
22	Across Rannoch Moor	Corrour railway station	34km	2	Harvey BMM Ben Nevis	Moderate
23	The Crianlarich Munros	Crianlarich	37km	2	OS Landranger 50, 51 & 56	Strenuous
24	Ben Vorlich from Glen Artney	Glen Artney	33km	2	OS Landranger 57	Moderate
25	Ben Lawers and Meall nan Tarmachan	Invervar	38km	2	OS Landranger 51	Strenuous

No	Walk Name	Start/Finish	Distance	Days	Maps	Difficulty
26	The Trossachs from Balquhidder	Balquhidder	38km	2	Harvey Superwalker Ben Ledi; OS Landranger 57	Moderate
27	The Munros of Glen Creran	Glen Creran	42km	2	Harvey BMM Ben Nevis	Strenuous
28	Ben Lomond and the shores of Loch Lomond	Rowardennan	42km	2	Harvey Superwalker (Ben Lomond)	Moderate
29	The East Coast of Islay	Port Askaig– Port Ellen	43km	2	OS Landranger 60	Moderate
30	Arran's High Hills	Brodick	43km	2	Harvey Superwalker (Arran)	Strenuous

Difficulty/Grade

Easy: Low level or short distances each day. Suitable for regular hillwalkers.

Moderate: Numerous hills or longer distances. Suitable for fit hillwalkers.

Strenuous: Multiple peaks traverses, or very long distances. Suitable for experienced Munro-baggers.

Challenging: Long mountain traverses, over difficult terrain. Suitable for experienced and fit mountain walkers.

APPENDIX 4
Glossary of Common Terms

The Gaelic and Old Norse places names often have a variety of spellings, and only the most common are given.

Munro	Mountain above 3000 feet (914.4m), originally a list drawn up by Sir Hugh Munro, but now much changed.
Corbett	Mountain between 2500 feet (762m) and 3000 feet (914.4m), with a drop on all sides of at least 500 feet (152.4m), originally drawn up by John Rooke Corbett.
Graham	Mountain between 2000 feet (610m) and 2500 feet (762m), with a drop on all sides of at least 150m, originally drawn up by Fiona Graham in 1992.

Abhainn	(Gaelic) river
Allt	(Gaelic) burn or stream
Aonach	(Gaelic) height
Ban	(Gaelic) white
Bealach	(Gaelic) col or mountain pass
Beag	(Gaelic) small
Beithe	(Gaelic) birch
Beinn	(Gaelic) hill
Breac	(Gaelic) speckled
Binnean	(Gaelic) peak
Bodach	(Gaelic) old man
Buidhe	(Gaelic) yellow
Cailleach	(Gaelic) old woman or witch
Carn	(Gaelic) hill or stones
Coinneach	(Gaelic) mossy place
Ciste	(Gaelic) chest or coffin
Clach	(Gaelic) stone
Coire	(Gaelic) cirque or upland valley or corrie
Creag	(Gaelic) crag
Dale	(Old Norse) valley
Damh	(Gaelic) stag

Dearg	(Gaelic) red
Dubh	(Gaelic) black
Eilean	(Gaelic) island
Fionn	(Gaelic) white
Fraoch	(Gaelic) heather
Garbh	(Gaelic) rough
Geal	(Gaelic) white
Geo	(Old Norse) break in the coast
Gleann	(Gaelic) glen or valley
Gorm	(Gaelic) blue
Inbhir (Inver)	(Gaelic) mouth of a river
Lairig	(Gaelic) hill pass
Loch	(Old Norse) lake
Lochan	(Old Norse) small loch or lake
Meall	(Gaelic) bare hill or lump
Monadh	(Gaelic) hill range
Mor	(Gaelic) big
Sgor	(Gaelic) rocky peak
Strath	(Gaelic) valley
Stob	(Gaelic) peak
Uaine	(Gaelic) green
Uisge	(Gaelic) water

NOTES

NOTES

NOTES

SAVE £££'s with
tgo
THE GREAT OUTDOORS

tgo
THE GREAT OUTDOORS
HILL WALKING • BACK PACKING
TREKKING • SCRAMBLING

INSIDE
Lakeland Passes
The best bits without the highest bits!
Night Hikes
Mountains & moors after dark
Against the Grain
Seasonal breaks, above Loch Treig

Wild Drovers
On the ancient trails of the cattlemen

PLUS: What to pack when winter comes howling in
Pyrenean Highways – hiking Europe's smallest state

November 2002 • £2.95

Britain's leading monthly magazine for the dedicated walker. To find out how much you can save by subscribing call

0141 302 7744

HILLWALKING • BACKPACKING • TREKKING • SCRAMBLING

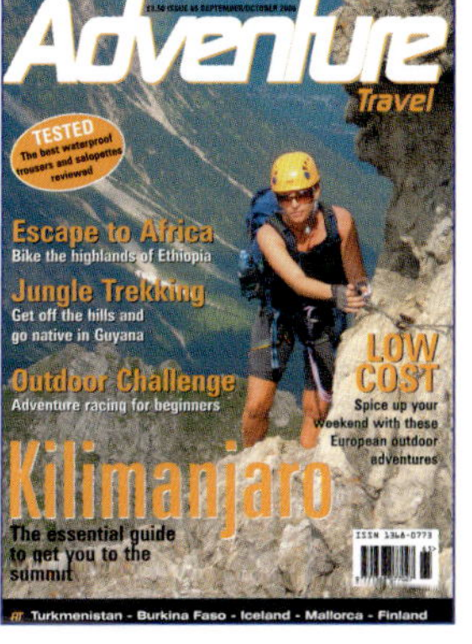

Get ready for take off

Adventure Travel helps you to go outdoors over there

More ideas, information, advice and entertaining features on overseas trekking, walking and backpacking than any other magazine - guaranteed.

Available from good newsagents or by subscription - 6 issues £15

Adventure Travel Magazine T:01789-488166

LISTING OF CICERONE GUIDES

BACKPACKING
Backpacker's Britain:
  Vol 1 – Northern England
  Vol 2 – Wales
  Vol 3 – Northern Scotland
  Vol 4 – Southern Highlands
Book of the Bivvy
End to End Trail
National Trails
Three Peaks, Ten Tors

BRITISH CYCLE GUIDES
Border Country Cycle Routes
Cumbria Cycle Way
Lancashire Cycle Way
Lands End to John O'Groats
Rural Rides:
  No 1 – West Surrey
  No 2 – East Surrey
South Lakeland Cycle Rides

CANOE GUIDES
Canoeist's Guide to the North-East

DERBYSHIRE, PEAK DISTRICT, EAST MIDLANDS
High Peak Walks
Historic Walks in Derbyshire
Star Family Walks Peak District and
  South Yorkshire
Walking in Peakland
White Peak Walks:
  Vol 1 – Northern Dales
  Vol 2 – Southern Dales

FOR COLLECTORS OF SUMMITS
Mountains of England & Wales:
  Vol 1 – Wales
  Vol 2 – England
Relative Hills of Britain

IRELAND
Irish Coast to Coast Walk
Irish Coastal Walks
Mountains of Ireland

ISLE OF MAN
Isle of Man Coastal Path
Walking on the Isle of Man

LAKE DISTRICT AND MORECAMBE BAY
Atlas of the English Lakes
Coniston Copper Mines
Cumbria Coastal Way
Cumbria Way and Allerdale Ramble
Great Mountain Days in the
  Lake District
Lake District Anglers' Guide
Lake District Winter Climbs
Roads and Tracks of the Lake District
Rocky Rambler's Wild Walks
Scrambles in the Lake District:
  North
  South
Short Walks in Lakeland:
  Book 1 – South
  Book 2 – North
  Book 3 – West

Tarns of Lakeland:
  Vol 1 – West
  Vol 2 – East
Tour of the Lake District
Walks in Silverdale and
  Arnside
Lakeland Fellranger:
  The Central Fells
  The Mid-Western Fells
  The Near-Eastern Fells
  The Southern Fells

MIDLANDS
Cotswold Way

NORTHERN ENGLAND LONG-DISTANCE TRAILS
Dales Way
Hadrian's Wall Path
Northern Coast to Coast Walk
Pennine Way
Teesdale Way

NORTH-WEST ENGLAND
Family Walks in the
  Forest of Bowland
Historic Walks in Cheshire
Ribble Way
Walker's Guide to the
  Lancaster Canal
Walking in the Forest of Bowland
  and Pendle
Walking in Lancashire
Walks in Lancashire Witch Country
Walks in Ribble Country

PENNINES AND NORTH-EAST ENGLAND
Cleveland Way and Yorkshire
  Wolds Way
Historic Walks in North Yorkshire
North York Moors
South Pennine Walks
Spirit of Hadrian's Wall
Yorkshire Dales – South and West
Walking in County Durham
Walking in Northumberland
Walking in the South Pennines
Walking in the Wolds
Walks in Dales Country
Walks in the Yorkshire Dales
Walks on the North York Moors:
  Books 1 and 2
Waterfall Walks – Teesdale and High
  Pennines
Yorkshire Dales Angler's Guide

SCOTLAND
Ben Nevis and Glen Coe
Border Country
Border Pubs and Inns
Central Highlands
Great Glen Way
Isle of Skye
North to the Cape
Lowther Hills
Pentland Hills

Scotland's Far North
Scotland's Far West
Scotland's Mountain Ridges
Scottish Glens:
  1 – The Cairngorm Glens
  2 – Atholl Glens
  3 – Glens of Rannoch
  4 – Glens of Trossach
  5 – Glens of Argyll
  6 – The Great Glen
Scrambles in Lochaber
Southern Upland Way
Torridon
Walking in the Cairngorms
Walking in the Hebrides
Walking on the Isle of Arran
Walking in the Ochils, Campsie Fells
  and Lomond Hills
Walking in the Orkney and the
  Shetland Isles
Walking the Galloway Hills
Walking the Munros:
  Vol 1 – Southern and Central
  Vol 2 – Northern and Cairngorms
West Highland Way
Winter Climbs – Ben Nevis and
  Glencoe
Winter Climbs – Cairngorms

SOUTHERN ENGLAND
Channel Island Walks
Definitive Guide to Walking
  in London
Exmoor and the Quantocks
Greater Ridgeway
Isles of Scilly
Lea Valley Walk
North Downs Way
South Downs Way
South West Coast Path
Thames Path
Walker's Guide to the Isle of Wight
Walking in Bedfordshire
Walking in Berkshire
Walking in Buckinghamshire
Walking in Dorset
Walking in Kent
Walking in Somerset
Walking in Sussex
Walking in the Thames Valley
Walking on Dartmoor

WALES AND WELSH BORDERS
Ascent of Snowdon
Glyndwr's Way
Hillwalking in Wales:
  Vols 1 and 2
Hillwalking in Snowdonia
Lleyn Peninsula Coastal Path
Pembrokeshire Coastal Path
Ridges of Snowdonia
Scrambles in Snowdonia
Shropshire Hills
Spirit Paths of Wales
Walking Offa's Dyke Path

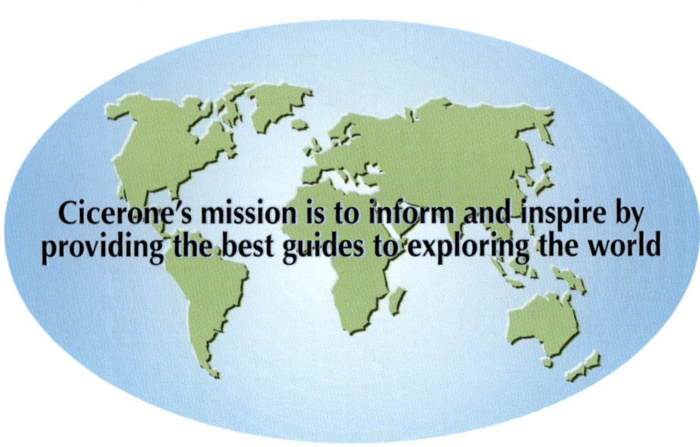

Since its foundation over 30 years ago, Cicerone has specialised in publishing guidebooks and has built a reputation for quality and reliability. It now publishes nearly 300 guides to the major destinations for outdoor enthusiasts, including Europe, UK and the rest of the world.

Written by leading and committed specialists, Cicerone guides are recognised as the most authoritative. They are full of information, maps and illustrations so that the user can plan and complete a successful and safe trip or expedition – be it a long face climb, a walk over Lakeland fells, an alpine traverse, a Himalayan trek or a ramble in the countryside.

With a thorough introduction to assist planning, clear diagrams, maps and colour photographs to illustrate the terrain and route, and accurate and detailed text, Cicerone guides are designed for ease of use and access to the information.

If the facts on the ground change, or there is any aspect of a guide that you think we can improve, we are always delighted to hear from you.

Cicerone Press
2 Police Square Milnthorpe Cumbria LA7 7PY
Tel: 015395 62069 Fax: 015395 63417
info@cicerone.co.uk www.cicerone.co.uk

CICERONE